365 WAYS to save the earth

Philippe Bourseiller

Preface by Elizabeth Kolbert

Text by Anne Jankéliowitch, Ariel Dekovic and Paula Tevis

Translated from the French by Simon Jones

Harry N. Abrams, Inc., Publishers

To Frédéric and Nicolas with all my heart
'You cannot stop a bird in flight...'

PREFACE

With an apparently incongruous combination of hard facts and stunning images, at first sight this book presents something of a contradiction. On each double page spread there is advice on everyday urban and suburban living – make sure you dispose of leftover paint properly, check your car's exhaust emissions, boil only as much water as you need when making tea or coffee – coupled with a spectacular photograph of the natural world taken by Philippe Bourseiller – Alaska's Denali massif, Hawaii's Kilauea volcano, Patagonia's Cerro Torre. While the text concerns the ordinary and everyday, the photographs portray the extraordinary beauty of nature.

However, what is striking about this apparent mismatch of factual advice and gorgeous images, is that they are not mismatched at all. How we go about our daily lives – what we eat, how we get to work, where we build our houses – has an effect not just on our immediate surroundings, but on places as far away as the North Pole and Antarctica. Spending the day moving from an air-conditioned home to a hermetically-sealed office block and back again, via an underground car park, it is all too easy to overlook this fact – but that is all the more reason why we must become aware of it. The food that we buy in the supermarket frequently originates halfway around the world; in buying it, we may be giving our unwitting consent to the destruction of faraway forests and indigenous cultures. Residue from the fertiliser that we apply to our lawns finds its way into streams and rivers, and then eventually into the sea, where it contributes to algae blooms that produce eutrophic 'dead zones' where no fish can survive. The water that we pump from underground aquifers cannot be replaced as fast as it is being drawn out – so the water that we waste today running half empty dishwashers will be lost to the future generations who will almost certainly need it.

Perhaps the clearest example of how our ordinary, everyday actions are altering the planet is global warming. One of the most astonishing places that Philippe Boursellier photographed for this book is Greenland, which, after Antarctica, is home to the world's largest ice sheet. Last summer, I also visited Greenland to interview scientists who were studying the effects of global warming on the ice. I spent a day in a village on Disko Bay, watching icebergs float out to sea. While I was there, I spoke to some native fishermen. They described how in recent years, they had seen the icebergs in the bay growing steadily smaller; instead of towering mountains of white that drifted around the ocean for weeks, the icebergs tended to be smaller and more likely to break up. They also told me that for as long as anyone could remember, the bay had remained frozen for several months each winter. During the last few years, however, there had been open water in Disko Bay all year long. The fishermen were alarmed by the change, as we all should be.

Sea ice reflects sunlight, while open water absorbs it. Vast stretches of Arctic sea ice are now disappearing, reducing, as they do so, the earth's ability to reflect some of the sun's light. The result is an intensifying of the global warming process caused by man, pushing us closer and closer to catastrophe. Scientists warn that if we do not take steps to curb emissions of greenhouse gases soon, not just the sea ice, but the Greenland ice sheet itself will start to melt, which would release enough water in total to raise global sea levels by seven metres.

Americans comprise just four per cent of the world's population, and yet they produce nearly a quarter of the world's greenhouse gas emissions, making the US contribution to the way the planet is changing quite considerable. Roughly three-quarters of all electricity in the US is produced by burning fossil fuels. Every time we switch on the light, turn on the coffee maker, or watch the news on TV, we are all adding to the problem, albeit indirectly. We contribute to it directly, however, whenever we get into the car. Probably the single-most important step anyone of us can take to reduce our emissions is to buy a fuel-efficient car, and then, whenever possible, to leave it in the garage. Global warming is not a problem that can be 'solved' by individual actions; it will require a concerted international effort, over decades.

Two of the themes to be found in Philippe Bourseiller's photographs are the power of nature and nature's vulnerability. Another apparent contradiction lies at the heart of this. The forces that have shaped the planet over millennia – volcanic eruptions, tectonic shifts – remain beyond man's influence. In Bourseiller's photographs, that tiny dot walking across the Greenland ice sheet or scaling Trou de Fer on Réunion is a human figure. Yet, at the same time, we humans, tiny as we are in the scale of things, have proved infinitely adept at wiping out species that have inhabited the planet since long before our own species evolved. We are now in the process of altering the chemistry of earth's atmosphere by burning fossil fuel deposits that were laid down during the age of the dinosaurs. Already, we have succeeded in raising carbon dioxide concentrations to a level higher than at any other point in the last three and a half million years. 'The lifetime of one human being is nothing on a geological scale, but the traces he leaves behind can be unbelievably destructive', as Philippe Bourseiller has observed.

For all their grandeur, the photographs collected in this book are elegiac. 'I do not change or transform reality', Bourseiller has said about his work. 'I am content with just seizing an instant of it. I hope my photographs help people become aware and fully conscious of the fact that these extraordinary landscapes which surround us are extremely fragile and that they must be protected constantly.'

Elizabeth Kolbert

CONTENTS

HOME

January : 2, 4, 5, 7, 13, 16, 18, 26, 28, 30

February : 1, 3, 6, 7, 10, 15, 17, 21, 23, 25, 28

March : 1, 10, 12, 14, 18, 23, 26, 28, 30,

April : 2, 7, 8, 17, 19, 22, 26, 28, 29,

May : 4, 5, 7, 13, 14, 17, 20, 22, 23, 25, 28, 30, 31

June : 1, 2, 5, 6, 7, 11, 13, 21, 22, 24, 26, 27, 30

July : 5, 8, 9, 18, 24

August : 1, 7, 9, 17, 21, 24, 28

September : 5, 6, 8, 14, 18, 21, 24, 25, 27, 30

October : 1, 3, 6, 9, 11, 12, 16, 17, 18, 20, 23, 30, 31

November : 5, 7, 8, 10, 11 ; 16, 18, 21, 29

December : 2, 5, 6, 8, 11, 14, 16, 17, 19, 28, 30

SHOPPING

January : 1, 8, 9, 12, 15, 17, 20, 22, 27, 31

February : 4, 16, 19, 22

March : 2, 5, 9, 11, 15, 19

April : 1, 3, 5, 15, 18, 23, 27

May : 2, 8, 9, 18

June : 12, 15, 16, 23, 28

July : 3, 6, 11, 17, 23, 25, 27, 28, 29

August : 3, 11, 19, 22, 23, 27

September : 2, 9, 11, 23, 26, 29

October : 8, 15, 21, 24, 29

November : 4, 9, 12, 15, 17, 19, 23, 26

December : 20, 24, 27, 29, 31

LEISURE

January : 10, 11, 24

February : 2, 5, 13, 14, 26

March : 3, 13, 16, 24, 29

April : 6, 13, 14, 16, 21, 25

May : 6, 12, 16, 19, 26, 27

June : 3, 8, 9, 14, 17, 19, 20, 29

July : 7, 10, 13, 14, 15, 16, 19, 20, 26, 31

August : 2, 6,14, 18, 20, 25, 26, 31

September : 1, 7, 13, 19, 28

October : 4, 7, 19, 26, 27

November : 6, 24

December : 12, 18, 22, 25, 26

TRANSPORTATION

January: 19, 23, 25

February: 11, 20

March: 4, 6, 8, 20, 31

April: 4, 11

May: 10, 21

June: 10, 18, 25

July: 2, 12, 22

August: 4, 5, 8, 13

September: 10, 22

October: 2, 14, 28

November: 2, 22, 27

December: 1, 7

CHILDREN

January: 6

March: 22, 27

April: 10

May: 1

June: 4

July: 21, 30

August: 10, 16, 29

September: 3, 16, 20

October: 10

November: 30

December: 15, 21, 23

OFFICE

January: 14, 21

February: 9, 18, 27

March: 7, 17

April: 9, 30

May: 15

July: 4

August: 30

September: 4, 15

October: 5, 13, 22, 25

November: 1, 3, 13, 14, 20, 28

December: 3, 9, 10

GARDENING

January: 3, 29

February: 8, 12, 24

March: 21, 25,

April: 12, 20, 24

May: 3, 11, 24, 29

July: 1

August: 12, 15

September: 12, 17

November: 25

December: 4, 13

Agriculture – Buy Fair Trade products, and help combat child labour.

Worldwide, some 211 million children between the ages of 5 and 14 are forced to work. Three-quarters of these children work in agriculture. Employed on plantations producing sugar cane, tea, tobacco and coffee, they often toil in fields that have been freshly sprayed with pesticides, sometimes even working while spraying takes place. Fair Trade labels guarantee that goods are produced under fair conditions, that workers are paid fairly, that forced labour is forbidden and, of course, that children are not used as a source of cheap labour.

Buying Fair Trade products is, among other things, a way of working towards safeguarding basic human rights, especially the rights of children.

Mount Benbow volcano, Vanuatu

Energy – Turn down your heating by 1°C.

Buildings are a major source of the greenhouse gases responsible for climate change. Two-thirds of the energy used by buildings is for hot water and heating. Carefully managing our domestic heating thus allows us to minimise global warming and to avoid further polluting the air around us.

Our houses are often heated to excess. The ideal living room temperature is 20°C, and bedrooms are healthier at 16°C. Each one-degree increase in temperature produces a 7 to 11 per cent increase in energy consumption (depending on how well-insulated your home is). Use your heat wisely and insulate well.

Whale shark, Australia

Forests – Recycle Christmas trees and cards.

As soon as Christmas is over, countless Christmas trees and Christmas cards are thrown out with the household waste. Disposing of them is costly for the community and is a needless waste of raw or recyclable materials. Some local authorities make arrangements for the collecting of trees and cards for recycling. Thanks to a campaign by the Woodland Trust, the UK's leading woodland conservation charity, 58 million Christmas cards were recycled following the festive season of 2004.

Recycle your cards and if your local authority does not collect Christmas trees, ask if it can arrange to do so. Buy a tree with its roots intact and plant it in a container. Keep it watered and when Christmas is over, plant it out in the garden.

Blizzard over the inlandsis, Greenland

january 4th

Energy – Buy 'green' electricity.

The Eugene standard (and its accredited certification labels), conferred by the European network of the same name, offers electricity producers, consumers, and governments simple, relevant criteria for assessing the environmental quality of a given electricity source, and to choose electricity supplies certified as coming from renewable, non polluting energy sources. It also gives consumers interested in energy matters information on where their electricity comes from, and allows them to find out about the environmental impact of their choices. Renewable energy has far less impact on the environment than fossil fuels and nuclear power.

Find out how you can buy green electricity.

Aurora borealis, Finland

january 5th

Energy – Improve the efficiency of your radiators.

The world's consumption of energy is producing vast amounts of pollution and waste. The nuclear industry in particular produces an enormous amount of waste. Today there are 438 nuclear power stations in the world, and a further 34 are being built, 20 of these in Asia. Between them they produce 17 per cent of the world's electricity – and 10,000 tonnes of nuclear waste per year, adding to the 200,000 tonnes already in existence.

To reduce your domestic energy consumption, make your radiators more efficient by placing reflective panels or sheets of aluminium foil behind them, this will bounce the heat back into the room.

Namib Desert, Namibia

Waste – Encourage your place of work to start composting waste.

Organic household waste can be converted into compost, a natural fertiliser that will increase the soil's ability to retain air and water, check erosion and reduce the need for chemical fertilisers. The compost is produced by the action of the micro-organisms present causing the waste to break down and decompose, one kilogram of organic waste produces around 300 grams of compost.

——————————

The composting of organic waste can benefit the whole community. Take the initiative and approach your children's school canteen or the kitchen at your workplace, and explain the ecological and economic advantages of composting waste. Even if they do not decide to compost waste, it might encourage them to think about the amount that is thrown out and come up with alternative solutions to the problem.

Klyuchevskoy volcano, Kamchatka, Russia

Water – Use less water when flushing the toilet.

Water that has been used for domestic purposes such as in dishwashers, showers or washing machines (excluding the toilet), is called 'greywater'. Comprising at last half of all residential wastewater, it can be used for other purposes, such as watering the garden. While ecologically oriented buildings in the US have installed greywater systems, they have yet to make an appearance in any number in the UK.

Place a bottle filled with sand in your toilet cistern and you will reduce the volume of water used with each flush. Do not use a brick (as is sometimes recommended) since if it starts to decay, pieces could get into the toilet system and cause leaks. Alternatively, replace your toilet with a low-flush or dual-flush type toilet. The half-flush option means that water use can be reduced by up to 8 litres for every flush.

Iceberg, Greenland

Consumption – Buy recycled.

Buy products that can be recycled in order to save natural resources. Recycled goods perform just as well as new products made from raw materials. Although some recycled goods are more expensive, many are competitively priced, particularly those products which have been on the market for some time. Be proactive and encourage recycling by buying more recycled products.

─────────

When you go shopping, always look for a recycled version of whatever you want to buy. Many kinds of products are now available: from office supplies, paper, textiles and carpets, to building materials and parts for your car.

Lagoons, Baja California, Mexico

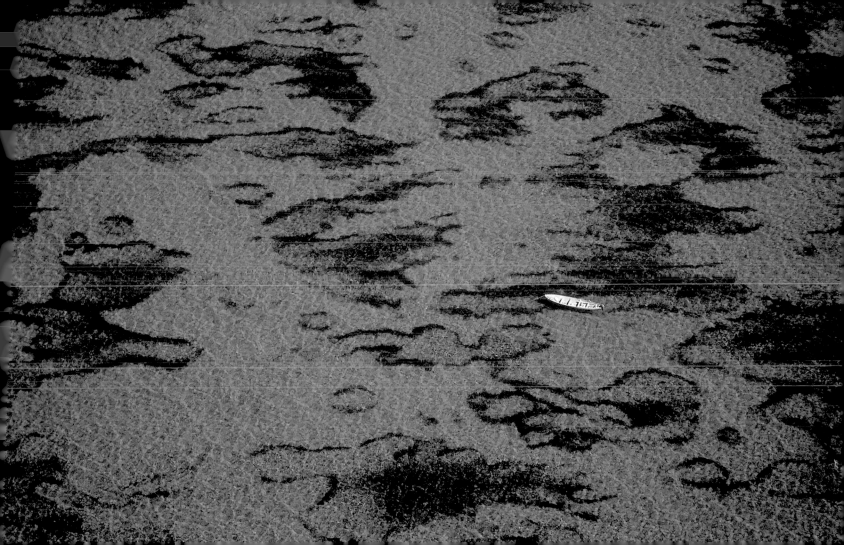

Agriculture – Make it a rule to buy organic for a given product.

To protect crops from parasitic insects and plants, farmers use pesticides, and to increase their crop yields, they spread fertilisers. World consumption of the chemicals used in both is growing exponentially: it leapt from 30 million tonnes a year in 1960 to 140 million tonnes in 2000. However, half the pesticides and fertilisers sprayed over fields are of no benefit to crops. As soon as it rains, the excess runs off into rivers and seeps into groundwater (from which two-thirds of our drinking water comes).

———————

Organic farming avoids the damage caused to the environment by pesticides and insecticides. Buy organic produce to encourage organic farming practices and in the interests of your own health – strawberries, apples and spinach, in particular, retain high levels of pesticide residue if produced non-organically.
www.organicconsumers.org/organic/pesticide-residues.cfm

Acacia, Namibia

Leisure – Be environmentally aware when taking part in your favourite leisure activity.

Many people take part in leisure activities that involve coming into direct contact with the environment. The careless and selfish attitude of some can cause enormous damage. Unscrupulous divers hack off pieces of beautiful coral to take home as souvenirs. What would become of the coral reef if all divers did this? A yachtsman might tip several litres of oil overboard while out at sea or sailing on a lake. What would happen if all yachtsmen disposed of used oil in the same way?

Respect nature and the environment when taking part in outdoor activities. Whatever your passion, whether it is climbing in the mountains, diving or sailing, there should be an environmental charter for your sport to encourage responsible behaviour. Contact your sport's national federation. If such a charter does not yet exist, suggest that one be drawn up.

Soft coral, Indonesia

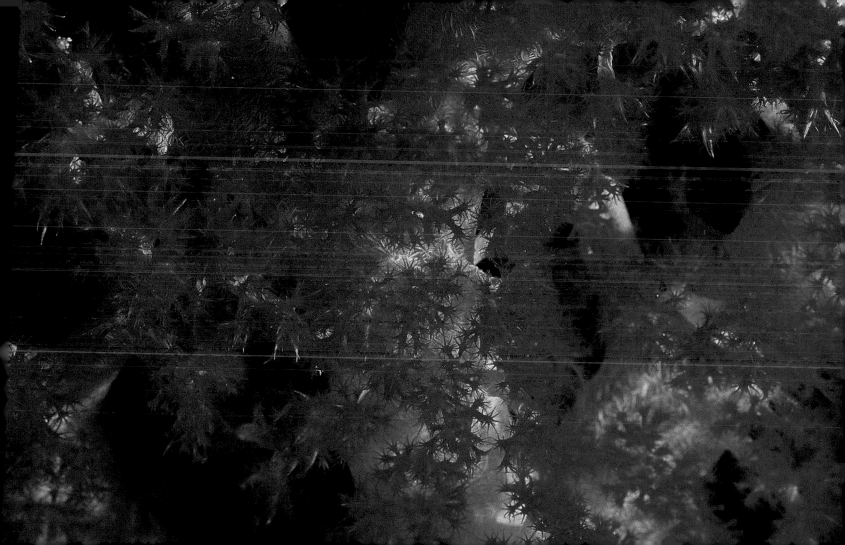

january 11th

Biodiversity – Do not feed wild animals.

Feeding wild animals, whatever kind they are and whatever their habitat, changes their diet and can alter their behaviour if it makes them accustomed to the presence of people, and dependent on receiving food instead of finding it themselves. Nor should you attempt to touch them, since it could endanger their health by exposing them to illnesses to which they are not immune – as well as put your own health at risk.

Be content to watch wild animals from a distance, without trying to attract them closer with food. Also, make sure that you put your own food and rubbish out of reach of wild animals, so that the bolder ones are not tempted to help themselves while you are not looking.

Marine iguanas, Galápagos Islands

january 12th

Lifestyle – Be an ethical investor.

Socially Responsible Investments (SRIs) are made in companies that take into account the social and environmental impact of their activities. Such investments support projects that encourage social integration and job creation, together with initiatives in areas such as ecology, renewable energy, Fair Trade products and organic food and farming. The SRI Compass website helps guide you through socially responsible investing in Europe.

_____

These investments generally carry as little risk as the non-ethical kind and are offered by various savings institutions; they include simple mutual funds, life insurance contracts and deposit accounts. There are enough ethical financial products on the market to suit all your investment requirements.
www.sricompass.org

Patagonia, Argentina

Energy – Use the refrigerator correctly to keep energy consumption down.

Refrigerators and freezers require large amounts of energy to chill and freeze foods. However, by taking a few sensible precautions you can keep their energy consumption down to an acceptable level. The temperature of the room in which the refrigerator or freezer is situated probably has the greatest impact on its energy consumption. The difference in the amount of electricity used by a refrigerator in a room at 15°C and one at 25°C can be as much as 10 per cent.

Do not position your fridge or freezer near a heat source, such as a cooker or radiator, or even a south-facing window. And take care not to put hot dishes inside the refrigerator or to overfill it. Both will lead to increased electricity consumption.

Hoarfrost, Sweden

january 14th

Waste – Coffee, milk, and sugar: say 'no' to individual portions.

Coffee sold in individual portions uses 10 times as much packaging as when you buy it in bulk. This extra packaging adds between 20 and 40 per cent to the cost of a product.

At your workplace, suggest that individual packets of coffee, sugar, cream and tea be replaced by large containers for everyone's use. It will be cheaper and will keep waste to a minimum. The environmental cost of individually packaged foodstuffs never bears any relation to their size.

Sandstone menhirs, Chad

january 15th

Chemicals – Use natural paints.

Many paints are a cocktail of chemicals. Avoid those that contain heavy metals (especially those made from lead, a lethal poison), Volatile Organic Compounds (VOCs), toxic organic pigments and antifungal compounds. Replace them with natural paints made from renewable resources such as plant oils (linseed, castor oil, rosemary and lavender) and minerals.

Choose beeswax, natural resins (such as pine), casein or chalk as binders, balsamic oil of turpentine or citrus distillates as solvents, and opt for vegetable pigments (valerian, tea, onion) or mineral (sienna, iron oxides). Just choose the colour you want.

Sand dunes, Algeria

Energy – Switch off any lights you do not need.

Greenhouses gases are naturally present in the atmosphere and help maintain the temperatures on earth that support life. However, an increase in these gases is leading to a warming of the global climate. During the course of the last century, global demand for energy increased by a factor of thirteen. Most of this energy, required for heating, lighting, etc., comes from the burning of oil, gas and coal, which produces greenhouse gases.

Make a point of switching off lights that do not need to be left on, particularly when you leave a room, and try to use daylight wherever possible. The less electricity you use, the less greenhouse gases will be pumped into the atmosphere in order to produce it.

Lava, Kilauea volcano, Hawaii

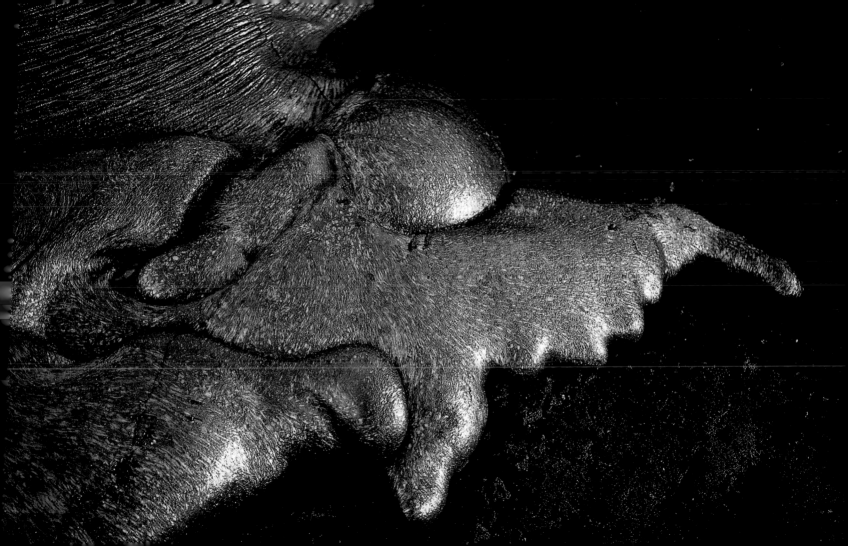

Energy – Check the energy efficiency rating when you buy household appliances.

The energy consumption of household appliances can vary a great deal depending upon the model. When you buy a new washing machine or freezer, check on the level of its energy consumption: you will save on your energy bill by doing so.

The European Energy label is an energy rating system that grades appliances on a scale from A to G, the A rating being the most efficient. When switched off, energy-efficient televisions use 3 watts of electricity less per hour than conventional televisions, which use 6 watts per hour. When it is time to replace an old appliance, always look for products with the European Energy label.

Piton de la Fournaise volcano, Réunion

Chemicals – Make use of old-fashioned household cleaning tips.

Chemicals have invaded our lives. Even in the 1980s, there were 500 times more chemical products available than there were during the 1940s. Today, an average family uses 20 to 40 litres of various kinds of chemical cleaner each year. These products, which are generally full of substances harmful to our health and the environment, inevitably find their way into water, air and soil.

It's time to take a leaf out of our grandmother's book and hark back to a time when cleaning products were much more natural: dishwashing detergent for oil stains, coal tar soap for grease stains, milk and lemon for ink, lemon juice for polishing copper, and many more...

Mud cauldrons, Kamchatka, Russia

Transport – Drive more slowly.

It has taken nature 250 million years to produce the earth's oil reserves, but the supply is likely to become exhausted at some time during the next century. Every American citizen uses the equivalent of 7.5 tonnes of petrol per year, while a European uses 3 tonnes and someone living in a developing country just half a tonne. The use of petrol and diesel for transport is continuing to increase at a rate of 4 per cent per year, but this increase masks certain inequalities. Annual consumption of petrol for use in cars in relation to the number of inhabitants is 30 litres in Africa, 50 litres in Asia, 430 litres in Western Europe and 1600 litres in North America.

Petrol efficiency declines rapidly when cars travel above 95 kph (59 mph), increasing both the cost of each trip you take and its environmental impact.

River, Iceland

Agriculture – Write to manufacturers urging them to keep genetically modified crops out of animal feed.

In 2003, 67 million hectares of transgenic crops were grown worldwide; about 60 per cent of these were in the United States. The global spread of genetically modified crops is not in response to a need for new varieties; it is dictated purely by the desire for short-term profits. Present labelling regulations do not require disclosure of products that come from animals that have been fed GM crops (such as meat, fish, eggs, dairy products, desserts, or pre-packaged meals). As much as 80 per cent of GM crops find their way into foodstuffs by this indirect route.

Write to farmers and distributors urging them to keep GM crops out of animal feed. In this way, you will help to keep them off your plate and protect the environment by discouraging their cultivation for animal feed.

Sea lion, Galápagos Islands

Waste – Choose 'draft' quality when printing.

Printer cartridges contain pollutants: aluminium, iron oxide and plastic. Luckily, they can easily be recycled. Even if damaged, defective parts can be recycled, and cartridges that are refilled are of equal quality to new ones. Ink powder, which is highly toxic, contains chemical pigments made from cyanide: if this finds its way into landfill sites, it will contaminate soil and water. During the recycling process, this ink powder is incinerated.

Reduce the pollution produced by ink cartridges by using less ink. Remember to choose 'draft' quality for all print jobs that do not require flawless print quality – and only print documents when necessary

Volcanic lake, Iceland

Transport of goods – Patronise local, independent shops.

In rich countries today, consumers travel by car to do their shopping in large malls built on the edges of urban areas. They store their food in freezers, the products taking up more space and therefore using more energy because they are sold in large quantities and with excess packaging. This system gives large retail organisations a high degree of control, which they use to force down farmers' prices or to import products from countries where labour is cheap and environmental legislation almost non-existent.

Use your local shops. Every new supermarket that opens causes hundreds of jobs in small independent shops to be lost. Pollution and congestion would be a quarter of current levels if consumers frequented their local shops, rather than travelling to large out-of-town shopping centres.

Pink flamingoes, Kenya

january 23rd

Waste – Dispose of old car batteries safely and correctly.

Car batteries contain lead and acid, substances that are extremely toxic to the environment. Left on wasteland, a battery will pollute the area immediately around it (up to 15 square metres) for several years. Today, the largest source of lead pollution is the car, and most of the pollution comes from car batteries.

Recycle your old car battery correctly. Check with your local authority for their advice. They might recommend that you take it to civic disposal site, or to a garage which collects them for recycling and safe disposal.

Lake Magadi, Kenya

Biodiversity – Support animal-friendly (or animal-free) circuses.

Wild animals used in circuses or travelling shows rarely live in humane conditions; they are often deprived of any kind of regular veterinary care, and are usually chained in one position for long periods of the day, with no opportunity to move about. Government legislation meant to protect these animals is actually ineffective and is rarely enforced. Add to that the transitory nature of circuses and prosecution of violators is rarely, if ever, pursued.

Do not visit circuses or travelling shows that keep wild animals in captivity.

Clown fish, Australia

Transport – Use public transport.

Air pollution is top of the list of problems caused by motor vehicles, followed by accidents, noise and the erosion of habitats, and damage to animal and plant life caused by the building of roads and motorways. Finally, 80 per cent of journeys in towns and cities are made by car. This congestion costs us dearly: air pollution reduces the life of the average European by 8.6 months.

Choose public transport whenever possible. A bus can take 40 single-passenger cars off the road.

Eruption of Mount Pinatubo, Philippines

Energy – Have your boiler serviced regularly.

Water for domestic use should never be heated above 60°C. Above that temperature, the excessive heat leads to limescale and the corrosion of pipes and other equipment. Limescale increases heating costs by insulating the water from the heating source, which means that more energy is needed to heat the water. In addition, a poorly maintained boiler can lead to air pollution inside the home.

To check whether your apparently harmless boiler is poisoning the air in your home, or contributing excessively to global warming, have it checked once a year.

Sea lion, Galápagos Islands

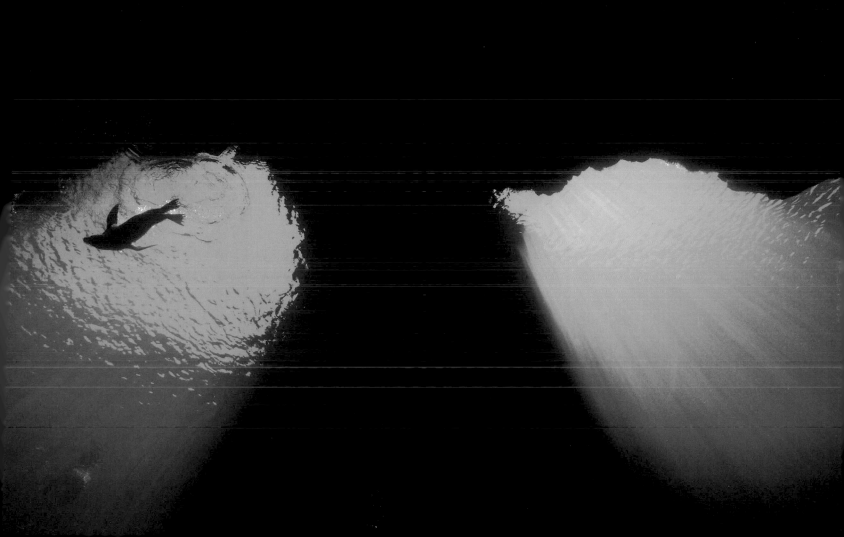

Consumption – Buy eco-labelled washing up liquids.

A quarter of the rivers and streams of Western and Southern Europe are severely polluted. Some are so badly degraded that they are considered biologically dead. It is now essential to treat our waste-water before returning it to the environment, in order to preserve the watercourses and groundwater from which we draw our drinking water supplies. However, this treatment cannot remove pollution completely and in addition, it produces a silt that must be disposed of. It is both easier and cheaper to pollute water less in the first place rather than to have to clean it up afterwards.

Choose eco-labelled washing up liquid. Among other advantages, it is largely biodegradable, less polluting to aquatic habitats and just as effective as less environmentally friendly kinds.

River, Iceland

Energy – Use residual heat to finish cooking your vegetables.

Climate change will have severe repercussions on plant and animal life, especially with species distribution. Many terrestrial species whose habitats will change will not be able to migrate quickly enough, or will not have enough time to adapt to new conditions. Climate change is therefore likely to threaten a quarter of the world's species directly. Certain studies have even suggested that by 2050 almost a fifth of species will have disappeared from the earth, even in the unlikely event that global warming is minimal.

In the kitchen, switch off the gas or electricity a few minutes before cooking is complete, and make use of the residual heat to finish cooking your vegetables.

Vulcano, Aeolian Islands, Italy

Waste – Put non-recyclable card and paper in the compost.

Reduce the volume of your rubbish by 80 per cent simply by sorting through your packaging, and composting all waste that is suitable. Leftover food, garden waste and other compostable items account for about a quarter of our annual waste.

———

Some kinds of non-recyclable paper and card (such as tissues, wipes, egg cartons) can be added to your compost. Their fibres will aerate the compost and help the organisms that cause decomposition.

Dwarf birches, Iceland

Waste – Reduce junk mail to reduce waste of raw materials.

Every year, 10 million trees, 15 billion litres of water and a considerable amount of energy are used in the production and disposal of junk mail. Thousands of tonnes of this mail ends up in landfills rather than in recycling bins.

Removing your name from a junk mail list can be as easy as sending a letter, postcard or email, or ticking a box on a form.

Icebergs, Greenland

Consumption – Be an ethical consumer.

The conditions for workers in developing countries, especially in Asian countries, are well documented. Some people work up to 80 hours per week, earning just a few cents per hour. It is impossible to continue to drive prices down and raise productivity indefinitely without abusing human rights or exploiting workers.

Buying a product means keeping the company that made it in business, implying approval of the conditions under which its employees work, supporting the way it makes its products and encouraging its environmental commitments – if they exist. Choosing your everyday purchases in a way that reflects the values of environmental and societal respect is one of the ways you can influence these organisations.

Murzuq *erg* (sand desert), Libya

Lifestyle – Keep within the law and observe regulations.

The UK has a whole arsenal of rules, regulations and legislation designed to protect the environment, from the protection of endangered species and threatened habitats, to the prevention of pollution, construction, industry, agriculture, fishing, and much more.

_____

If more people were to observe the law, far less damage would be inflicted upon the world. Ensure that you always observe environmental regulations.

Wayana Indians, Guyana

Biodiversity – Take part in a bird population census.

The British Trust for Ornithology runs a number of annual national surveys that provide information on the bird populations in various habitats. Since 1962, thousands of volunteer birdwatchers have participated in the Common Bird Census, which tracks the decline in species such as the song thrush and skylark. Additional censuses provide information on numbers, population trends and migration.

Give a little of your time to help with the next census. Apart from making a valuable contribution to the national bird survey, you might learn how to recognise wrens, robins, blackbirds and perhaps the grey partridge or linnet.

Sparrow, Galápagos Islands

february 3rd

Water – Turn off the tap while you clean your teeth.

The earth is nicknamed the 'blue planet', but this title is misleading. The supplies of fresh water are under severe pressure from the world's increasing population. There may be an abundance of water in the world's oceans, but fresh drinking water is in short supply. These reserves are not flexible, they cannot be expanded and yet they must be shared between an ever greater number of people.

By not letting the tap run while you clean your teeth, assuming the tap is left to run for 3 minutes, you will save almost 19 litres of water. That is more than someone in Kenya uses in a whole day.

River, Iceland

Biodiversity – Switch to recycled paper.

Almost half of the earth's original forests have disappeared, and only 20 per cent of these forests remain large enough to maintain their biodiversity. Every year more than 11 million tonnes of paper and cardboard are consumed in the UK, 85 per cent of which is imported, much of it from Scandinavia. In order to satisfy our increasing demand for wood and paper products, the majority of the natural boreal forest in Scandinavia has been converted into intensively managed secondary forest or plantations, where the inhabitants of a true and complex forest eco-system struggle to survive. About 5 per cent of Scandinavian old-growth forest remains, and yet this is still being logged.

Think about switching to alternative sources for your paper products, including 100 per cent recycled paper or paper made with agricultural waste. There are many companies producing paper from sources other than wood from which to choose.

http://www.paper.org.uk/

http://www.rethinkpaper.org/

Kokerbooms (or 'quiver trees'), Namibia

Biodiversity – Do not drop litter in the mountains.

The slopes of Mount Everest, the highest point on earth, have become well trodden over the past few decades. Up to 300 climbers a day gather at base camp during the peak season and the area has suffered considerable pollution as a result. Recently, several clean-up campaigns have relieved the 'roof of the world' of piles of rubbish; the first operation removed 27 tonnes of waste from the base camp areas. Mont Blanc in the French Alps, with some 3,000 climbers trampling across it every year, has suffered the same fate. Between 1999 and 2002, clean-up operations removed almost 10 tonnes of waste from the summit. High mountain peaks are extremely fragile environments, sensitive to the slightest disturbance and are easily damaged by mass tourism.

Do not contribute to the degradation of the mountains: take all your belongings, especially litter, with you when you leave and pick up what others have left behind irresponsibly.

Cerro Torre, Argentina

february 6th

Water – Do not leave the tap running while you wash dishes by hand.

The average person in the UK uses about 150 litres of water per day. In developing countries, the amounts used per person vary between one fifth and one twentieth of that. Each time we turn on the tap, a large part of the water goes into the drain without even being dirtied.

When you do the washing-up by hand, fill the sink rather than wash each plate under a continuously running tap. Also, turn off the tap while soaping your hands, shaving, washing the car, or hand-washing clothes. When a tap is turned on, depending on the force of the water, 19 to 57 litres of pure drinking water flow out every minute.

Inlandsis, Greenland

february 7th

Waste – Prepare glass bottles for recycling.

On average, British families use 330 glass bottles each year, and total glass use is estimated at 3.6 million tonnes annually. If we were to recycle this glass, for each tonne recycled we would save 603 kilograms of sand, 196 kilograms of soda ash, 196 kilograms of limestone and 68 kilograms of feldspar.

─────────────

Sort through your glass for recycling. Remove cork, plastic and metal lids, and rings from bottles, and make sure that windowpanes, light bulbs, mirrors, Pyrex items, porcelain and earthenware go into the bin. These are not recyclable and they will 'contaminate' your recycling collection.

Air bubbles trapped in ice, Canada

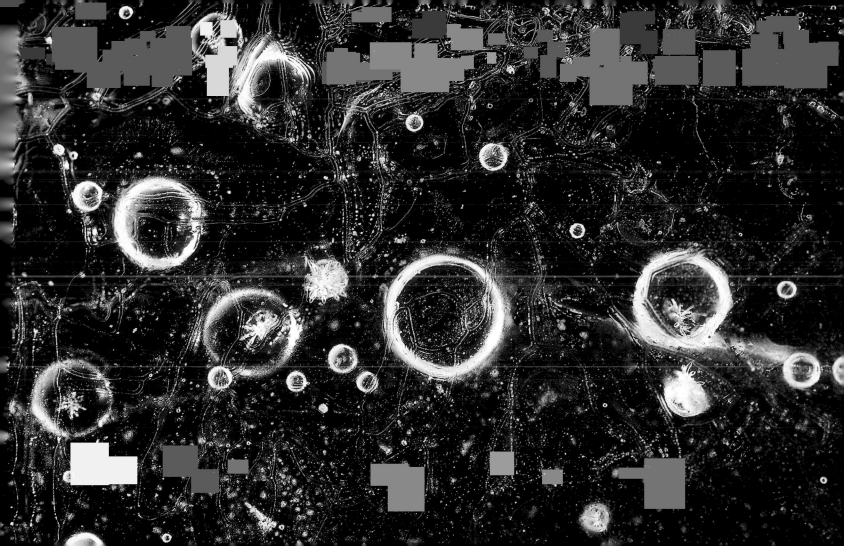

Water – Collect rainwater.

Rainwater is free. As with wind- and solar-powered energy, rainwater is one way to help protect the environment in a sustainable way. If we were to catch all the rain that falls on to the roofs of our homes, it would provide up to 80 per cent of current annual domestic water consumption. Collecting rainwater prevents it from picking up pollutants from the street before it enters storm drains and subsequently our water supply. Rainwater collection serves two purposes – it conserves water and helps to protect the environment from pollutants.

Rainwater collection does not have to be complicated, A simple water butt beneath a downpipe attached to guttering can collect considerable quantities – use it to water the garden or wash the car.

Sossusvlei dunes, Namibia

Lifestyle – Make the best use of technology to reduce the amount of journeys that you make.

To reduce the risk of climate change, the concentration of carbon dioxide in the atmosphere would need to be reduced by one-third to one-half of current emissions. This statistic means that the Kyoto Protocol, viewed as too demanding by the United States, the world's chief producer of greenhouse gas emissions, falls far short of what is needed to stabilise our global climate.

Reduce the amount of journeys that you make a week (keeping your costs down too) and save time by using the Internet or telephone when dealing with the bank or insurance company.

Erta Ale volcano, Ethiopia

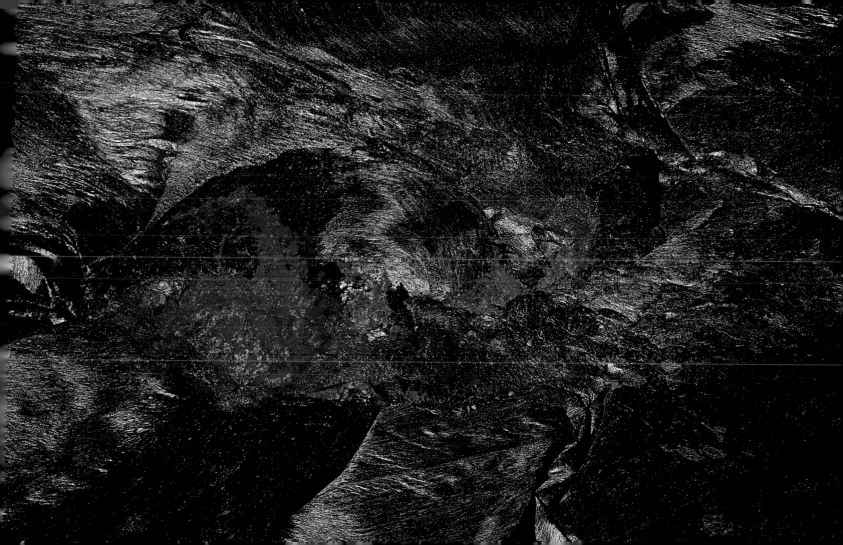

Waste – Sort actively and effectively; make inquiries.

When taking part in your local recycling programme, take note of the collection times, and get guidance from your local authority on how to sort it. Recycling is very worthwhile, but to be effective, waste needs to be sorted carefully.

If you are unsure what to do with a particular item of waste, put it in the non-recyclables, as putting it in the wrong bin makes life more complicated at the recycling centre. If your local authority does not yet offer waste-sorting facilities, take your waste to a recycling centre yourself.

Close-up of coral, Thailand

Transport – Warm up your car engine by driving off straight away.

One of the gases that contributes most to the greenhouse effect is carbon dioxide. Since 1900, emissions of carbon dioxide have risen by 12 times as a result of the growing consumption of coal, oil and gas. Its concentration in the atmosphere is the highest that it has been in the last 20 million years. On average, someone living in America causes twice as much carbon dioxide to be emitted as someone living in Japan, and 20 times as much as someone living in India. However, carbon dioxide emissions in developing countries will rise considerably in the coming decades.

A car engine warms up faster when it is being driven than when it is idling. When you start your car in the morning, drive off gently straight away. The engine will soon warm up and you will avoid needless pollution, carbon dioxide emissions and fuel consumption.

Lava cliffs, Hawaii

Waste – Report illegal dumping.

Illegal dumping, also known as 'fly tipping' is a growing problem in the United Kingdom. Illegal dumping is estimated to occur every 35 seconds somewhere in Britain and it costs the government millions to clear up. It should concern everyone, since often illegal dumping is considered a 'gateway' act: if it is tolerated in a particular area in a community, it sends a message that other illegal activities might also be tolerated. Bulky waste can also contain dangerous substances, which can pollute the soil, water and air, as well as being a blight on the landscape.

If you notice illegal dumping happening in your neighbourhood, take note of its location, the surrounding environment and type of waste, and report it to your local authority. They have the power to have it removed, even from private land.

Merapi volcano, Indonesia

The sea – Protect mangrove trees.

The mangrove forests that grow in swampy areas are a unique and important habitat for marine life and play a significant part in the functioning of local economies as well. They provide a refuge and spawning ground for fish and crustaceans, and also protect the shore line by trapping the sediment that is washed down by rivers and slow down the erosion caused by waves. Today, mangroves cover almost a quarter of tropical coastline. They used to cover half as much again, but are receding due to felling for wood, pollution and, increasingly, the expansion of shrimp farming (especially in Asia, which produces 80 per cent of the world's farmed shrimp). Half of the mangroves remaining are now considered degraded in some way. The impact of the destruction of mangroves on the ecosystem in coastal areas was recently found to be even more serious, when scientists discovered that they also provide spawning grounds for some coral reef fish species.

Avoid eating farmed shrimp, especially when staying in a foreign country.

Islets, Galápagos Islands

Agriculture – Give a potted plant as a gift, rather than a bunch of flowers.

A bunch of flowers bought from the florist or the supermarket might have been grown in a greenhouse thousands of miles away. Aside from the issue of transport over long distances, the boom in horticulture in some developing countries has had a high social and environmental cost. In Colombia, the flower industry uses enormous quantities of polluting pesticides, exposing poorly paid garden workers to chemicals that are sometimes carcinogenic or toxic. Elsewhere, as in Kenya, where water is scarce, horticulture requires substantial amounts of water and as a result, plunders local water resources.

When you wish to present someone with a bunch of flowers, choose a potted plant from a local supplier instead (and even better, choose one that has been grown organically). It will last far longer.

Tulip, France

Lifestyle – What is sustainable development?

By 2050, the earth will be home to almost 3 billion more people than it is today, most of them living in developing countries. How will the earth's natural resources be able to cope with the economic growth of these countries as well as that of industrialised nations? Governments will need to adopt less polluting manufacturing methods that use less energy and water. They will also need to look at conserving and sharing resources with other nations to create a fairer world, and consuming less and in smarter, more efficient ways. This is the principle of sustainable development – meeting the needs of the present without jeopardising the capacity for future generations to meet theirs.

If somebody asks you: What is sustainable development? Now you can explain and think about how you can make a difference!

Coral island, Australia

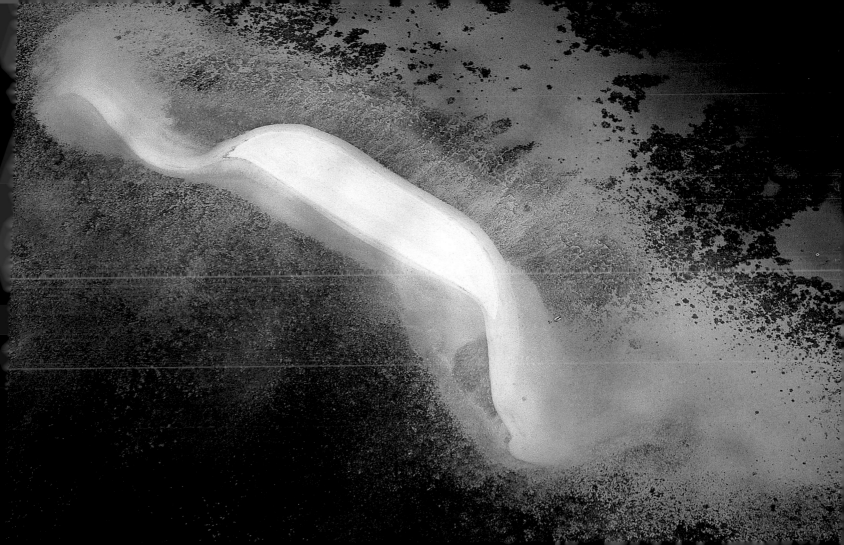

Transport of goods – Look at where the food you buy comes from.

Everyone knows that cars cause pollution, but we forget that food frequently travels long distances too, in order to reach our shops. The environmental impact of transporting food is considerable: the greater the distance it travels, the greater the emission of greenhouse gases.

To minimise this waste of resources and pollution, check the label for the origins of the fruit and vegetables you buy. Check to see what is in season in your area and find a local farmers' market or supplier. Food that is consumed in season should taste much better.

Dune, Mauritania

Energy – Insulate your home.

Even if you do not drive a car, you can take action to reduce climate change: an average home produces, through its consumption of energy (for hot water, heating, electricity and lighting), 6 tonnes of carbon dioxide per year – more than a car does. In Europe, about a quarter of all emissions of carbon dioxide, the main greenhouse gas responsible for climate change, comes from homes.

To reduce the need for heating, prevent heat from escaping: insulate the roof, floors, and walls with fibreglass wool, rockwool, or mineral wool cork, cellulose (from recycled newspapers), or hemp. This will save 20 per cent on your heating bills, and will pay for itself within 5 years at most.

Iceberg, Greenland

Waste – Recycle paper.

For many of us, the idea of recycled paper is associated with that of saving trees. However, this process allows us also to save water and energy, which are equally precious resources, and to reduce pollution. Every tonne of recycled paper saves 17 trees, 20,000 litres of water, and the energy equivalent of 1,000 litres of oil.

Today, less than 15 per cent of the paper used in offices is recycled. There is considerable room for improvement. Mention it at work, so that a used-paper collection programme may be implemented.

Acacia tree, Mali

Transport of goods – Buy local produce.

A kiwi fruit grown in New Zealand and transported to Europe by air involves the emission of 5 times its own weight in carbon dioxide. Kiwi fruits and similar 'exotic' produce are affordable in our shops and supermarkets because their prices do not reflect the hidden environmental and social costs.

————————

Look at where your food comes from: green beans from Kenya, carrots from Israel and apples from Australia are sold cheaply and do not reflect the true cost of their transport. Choose local produce: by supporting local farmers, you will be helping to reduce climate change.

Cranberries, United States

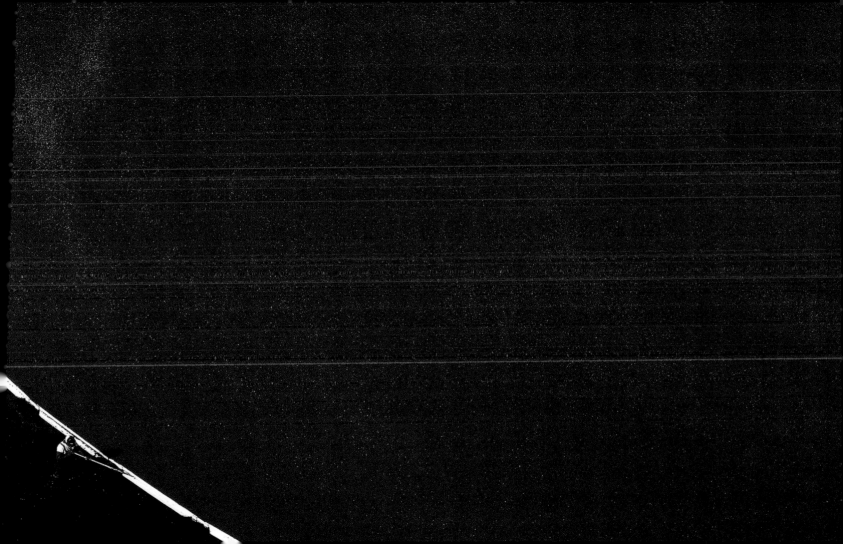

Transport – Look at an alternative to the conventional car – choose a Hybrid car.

Hybrid cars combine an electric motor with a conventional car engine. They run on electricity in town and use petrol out of town when the batteries are recharged while you are driving. Thanks to this efficient use of energy, Hybrid cars offer excellent performance and are much cleaner in town; they produce 75 per cent less pollution than standard vehicles. The Toyota Prius is already on the market and is extremely popular.

Hybrid cars are costly at present, but the price will fall when they are produced in large numbers.

Caymans, Venezuela

Water – Have low-flow showerheads fitted.

Rivers are dammed and diverted from their natural course in order to provide us with energy: 60 per cent of the world's rivers are used in this way and more than 45,000 barriers or dams enable 20 per cent of the world's water to be stored behind them. But the construction of these dams has displaced between 40 and 80 million people – few of whom were consulted beforehand – and has caused extensive deforestation and species loss. Harnessing the power of water involves heavy environmental cost.

You can cut your water consumption by replacing your showerhead with one that aerates and increases the flow of the water, producing a finer spray. The low-flow showerhead uses 7.5 litres per minute less than a conventional showerhead.

Islet, Iceland

Lifestyle – Invest in socially responsible companies.

One in five adults worldwide can neither read nor write. Of these, 98 per cent are in developing countries, and two thirds are women. In 2001, in sub-Saharan Africa, almost one in every 10 people aged between 15 and 24 was infected with HIV, and 2.4 million people died of AIDS. In 1966, Indira Gandhi pointed out that the greatest source of pollution on earth was poverty. And yet, 4 per cent of the wealth accumulated by the 225 richest people in the world could educate, feed and provide medical treatment for the entire population of the world.

Reward those companies that acknowledge that they can help to alleviate the inequalities in society – invest in socially responsible companies.

Bacteria, Kamchatka, Russia

Air – Have your heating system checked and maintained regularly.

Air pollution is obvious when you are sitting in the middle of a traffic jam. However, once indoors, you are still not safe from harmful emissions – especially carbon monoxide. This gas is produced by the incomplete combustion of coal, wood, gas or fuel oil, which can be caused by a blocked flue, the use of old or badly maintained cookers, boilers, or oil heaters, or clogged ventilation ducts preventing air circulation. Carbon monoxide poisoning kills up to 50 people in the UK each year.

Keep the air in your home clean: have your heating equipment checked and maintained by professionals – including the ventilation ducts or chimneys in your home.

White Desert, Egypt

Waste – Make compost with organic waste.

In nature, compostable waste (such as that found on the forest floor) decomposes into soil through the action of micro-organisms, returning energy and nutrients to the forest floor. Household rubbish contains a large amount of organic waste, which, instead of being returned to nature, is added to landfill sites.

———————

Leaves, branches, and grass from the garden, eggshells, fruit and vegetable peelings, coffee grounds, teabags and bread can all join the compost heap. After a number of weeks, if mixed well and regularly aerated, stirred to avoid clumping, and kept sufficiently moist, the result will be an excellent natural fertiliser.

Tundra, Russia

Lifestyle – Take legal action if necessary.

Environmental agencies tasked with protecting and restoring the environment sometimes fail to do so, occasionally out of negligence, but more frequently due to lack of funding. Make sure that your local politicians don't put environmental issues at the bottom of their list of priorities – human health and safety is at stake. Keep informed about the government's plans for care of the environment and monitor the trend in funding for environmental programmes.

___

If you want action on environmental issues, approach a pressure group. If you feel an organisation or government body is not complying with environmental regulations, make your feelings known and make a complaint.

Anaconda, Venezuela

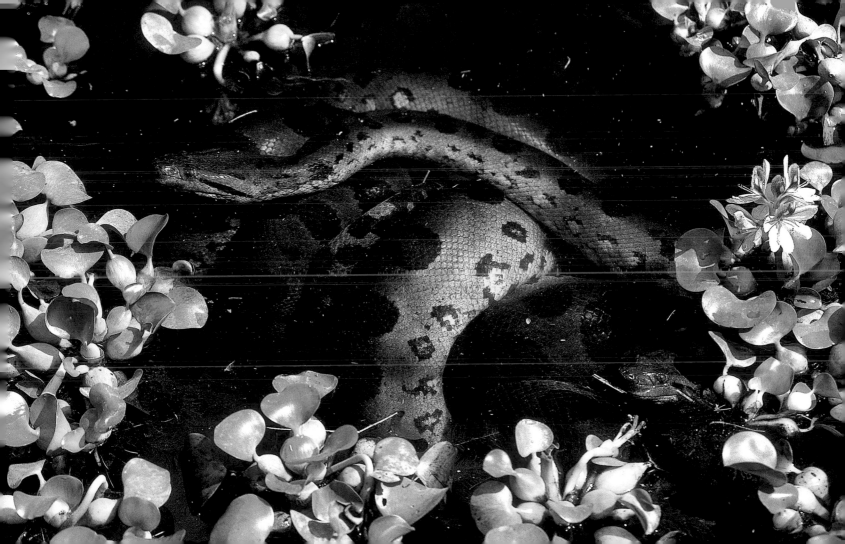

Waste – Do not drop your rubbish indiscriminately when travelling.

Depending on its type and where you live, domestic waste is sent to different destinations. In the UK, 84 per cent ends up in landfill sites, while 8 per cent is incinerated and 7 per cent is recycled or composted. Worldwide, only 20 per cent of household waste is treated in one of these ways. In some poor countries, rubbish bins are a rare sight or are never seen at all.

Do not drop rubbish, especially if you are on an excursion – even if the environment is already dirty or strewn with dumped waste. Take it back to where you are staying, and dispose of it there.

Volcanic cone, Iceland

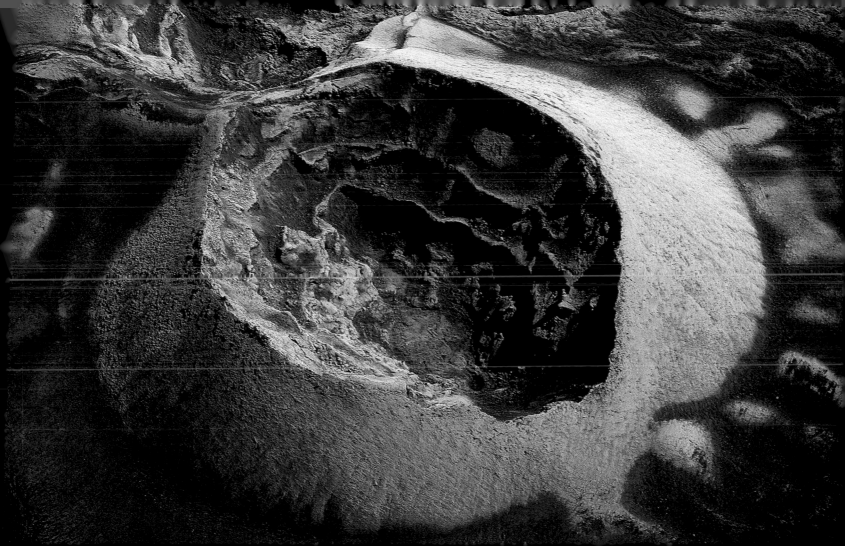

Waste – Choose your materials wisely.

A recent study showed that if 10 million office workers were to use one less staple a day, replacing it with a paper clip, 120 tonnes of steel would be saved in one year. Every tonne of recycled steel packaging saves 1.5 tonnes of iron ore, 0.5 tonnes of coal, 40 per cent of the water required in production, and 75 per cent of the energy needed to produce steel from virgin material.

––––––––––

With steel and other materials – especially those that cannot be recycled, such as certain plastics – get into the habit of buying something new only if there is no reusable alternative.

Humpbacked whales, Polynesia

february 28th

Energy – Do not defrost in the microwave.

Renewable energy – which comes from the sun, wind, the heat under the earth's crust, waterfalls, tides, the growing of vegetables or the recycling of waste – is infinite. Harnessing it produces little or no waste or polluting emissions. In countries like Germany, government officials have recognised the benefits of investing quickly and heavily in these technologies – their goal is the transition to 100 per cent renewable energy, including the reduction of their energy needs by 37 per cent.

Rather than adding to your electricity bill by using the microwave to defrost your food, remember to take it out of the freezer earlier and let it defrost at room temperature.

Erg (sand desert), Mauritania

Energy – Only boil the water you need.

Whether you use an electric kettle or a saucepan, heating water uses energy. There is no point in doubling the energy you use, for no purpose: only boil what is necessary. A British study found that if everyone in Britain did this on just one day, the energy saved could power the whole country's street lamps throughout the following night.

When you boil water for tea or a hot drink, try to boil only what you need – or pour the surplus into a Thermos flask, which will keep the water hot for the next cup.

Lake Assal, Djibouti

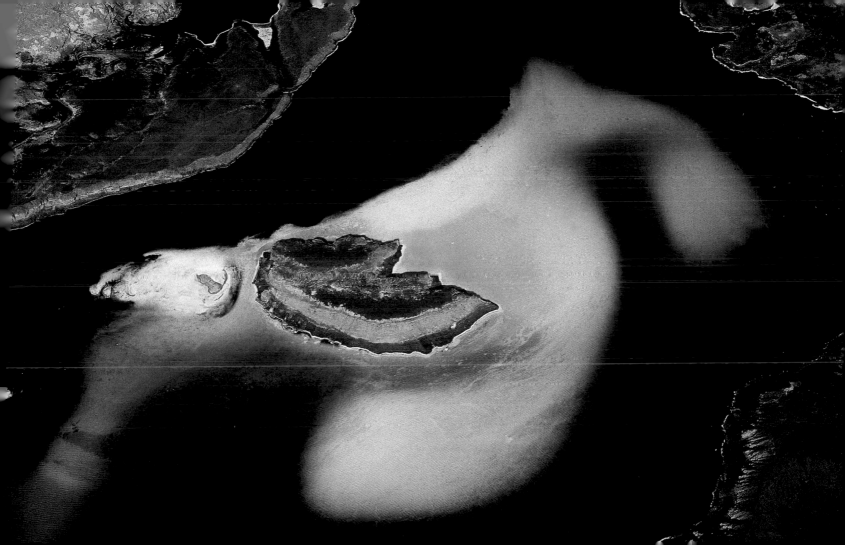

The sea – Avoid eating fish that has been farmed.

At present, fish farming accounts for 30 per cent of the world's fish production. However, it does not offer the diversity of species that are found naturally in the oceans: 300 species of fish are farmed, whereas 19,000 exist in the wild. In addition, in order to produce a farmed salmon weighing 3 kilograms, 15 kilograms of fish are caught in the wild to provide meal and oil. And, like all intensive farming, fish farming uses chemicals and antibiotics, which therefore enter the food chain to be consumed by people too.

In order to discourage intensive fish farming, which only exhausts the ocean's stocks further, avoid eating farmed fish such as seabass, salmon and trout.

Rhinopias aphanes, Australia

The sea – All water ends up in the sea, so be careful not pollute the water that enters drains.

All towns in the UK are equipped with wastewater treatment plants or have access to a plant nearby. However, at present, only 10 per cent of the world's urban environments have these plants. In most places, wastewater flows directly into rivers and the sea. Even rainwater, which picks up toxic substances such as oil, salt and pesticides as it falls onto streets and buildings, adds to the contamination of the sea. It can also cause sewers to overflow. Terrible though oil spills are, they are not the worst of the pollutants in the ocean.

Bear in mind that three-quarters of the sea's pollution originates on the land. So avoid polluting the streets and drains and try to use as few chemicals as possible in your garden.

Laguna Colorada, Bolivia

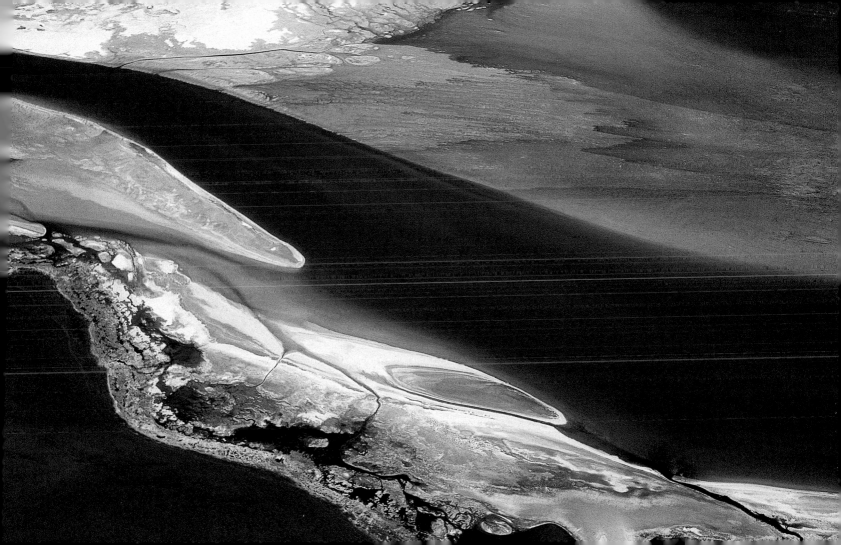

Waste – Dispose of your used engine oil properly.

Engine oil contains substances that are toxic to health and to the environment, especially heavy metals (lead, nickel, and cadmium). A third of used oil is refined to make new lubricants, and the remaining two thirds is used as fuel, chiefly in cement works. Only about 25 per cent of domestic waste oil is recycled. Estimates suggest that up to 35,000 tonnes of used engine oil is poured down the drain or is dumped illegally by DIY motorists who change their own oil.

Recycling old oil saves raw materials and energy, and saves the environment from yet more pollution. It also lessens our dependence on the vanishing oil reserves. It takes one barrel of crude oil to produce 2.4 litres of new engine oil, but it takes less than 4 litres of used engine oil to produce the same amount of high quality engine oil. Engine oil is collected at waste recycling centres and garages. Always take your old oil there.

Volcanic lake, Kamchatka, Russia

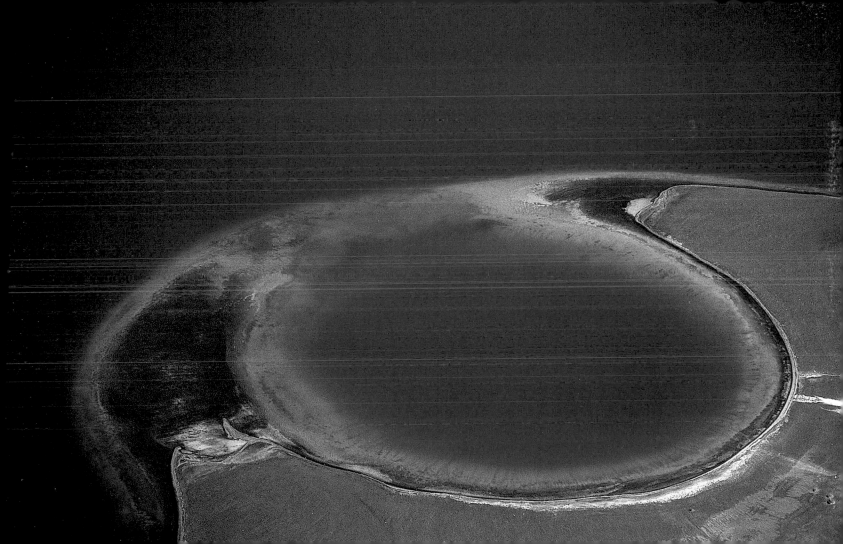

Energy – Do not use the pre-wash cycle on your washing machine.

Worldwide, 80 per cent of the energy consumed comes from the burning of fossil fuels – oil, coal and natural gas – which emit polluting gases and increase the greenhouse effect. Renewable energy, which comes from natural sources, only accounts for a small fraction of the energy used. Yet, it is inexhaustible and non-polluting: a wind turbine saves 1,000 tonnes of greenhouse gases per year. The European Union has announced that by 2010, 10 per cent of its electricity must come from renewable sources.

As we await the arrival of this cleaner energy, we should not delay consuming less now. Today's washing machines, which are highly efficient, allow you to bypass the pre-wash cycle, and thus save 15 per cent of the energy normally used.

Kilauea volcano, Hawaii

Transport – Consider getting rid of your car.

The toxic fumes emitted by industry and motor vehicles contain nitrogen dioxide (NO_2) and sulphur dioxide (SO_2). In the air, these compounds are converted into nitric acid and sulphuric acid, and then fall back to earth in rain. Acid rain eats away at the stone of historic buildings, destroys forests, acidifies lakes and rivers and attacks crops. Atmospheric pollution has done more damage to the Acropolis in Athens in 25 years than natural erosion has done in 25 centuries.

If you live in a large city and use your car only occasionally, consider renting a car, short- or long-term. It often works out more to be more economical once you take into account the cost of purchase, depreciation, insurance, parking space and possible fines.

Glacial corridor, United States

Waste – Do not throw out reusable paper products.

Europe, Japan and North America, home to just 20 per cent of the world's population between them, swallow up 63 per cent of all paper and cardboard produced. Consumption of these products is growing relentlessly: the richest countries use 3 times more of it today than in the 1960s. Over the next decade, the volume of paper used worldwide could grow by 40 per cent.

To avoid contributing to this over-consumption, cut back on your paper use and keep all your reusable paper products such as manila and file folders. Cut scrap paper into quarters and use it to write phone messages, rather than on a new pad. Similarly, keep reusable paper clips, elastic bands and binders in a drawer. And choose rewritable CD-ROMS – you will use fewer of them.

Mehedjibat *erg* (sand desert), Algeria

Transport – Calculate the greenhouse gas emissions that your journey by air produces.

Aircraft account for 13 per cent of the world's transport-related carbon dioxide emissions released into the atmosphere each year.

If you want to calculate how many greenhouse gas emissions will be produced during your next plane journey, check it out on the Internet where there are websites devoted to this purpose. A transatlantic flight produces almost half as much carbon dioxide as the average person produces in meeting all their other needs (lighting, heating and car travel) over a year.

Sea of clouds, Indonesia

Agriculture – Avoid a second Aral Sea.

Uzbekistan once contained the world's fourth largest inland sea – the Aral Sea. Today, the Aral Sea is 25 per cent of its original size. Since 1960, its waters have retreated by nearly 80 kilometres, leaving the region's fishermen, who once used to land 45,000 tonnes of fish per year, high and dry. By the late 1970s, the town of Moynaq, once a prosperous fishing town, was no longer anywhere near the shore. What was the cause of this ecological disaster? During the 1960s, the two great rivers that fed the sea were partially diverted to irrigate the region's cotton fields. The land was not meant to support this type of agriculture, the sea dried up and the soil, contaminated by salt and pesticides, turned to desert.

Cotton can be grown without causing ecological devastation. Organic cotton grows for a minimum of 3 years without chemical pesticides, defoliants, or fertilisers. Organic cotton is also processed without the use of harmful chemicals. You can encourage its production by choosing clothes made from organic cotton; if the thought of buying organic cotton products for your entire family is too daunting, start with the products your children wear.

Acid lake, Kamchatka, Russia

Air – Ventilate your home regularly.

Indoor air pollution affects all enclosed spaces. This particular form of pollution can be caused by a number of things: a ventilation system that does not remove stale air properly, a faulty gas cooker or heater, or the improper use of products such as paints, varnishes and household cleaners that require a high amount of air circulation to dissipate their pollutants. Some pollutants are natural in origin, such as dust mites and spores from mould.

On average, we spend 80 per cent of our time inside. The quality of the air indoors can therefore have a major effect on our health. To circulate the air and remove pollutants, ventilate your indoor space regularly and generously, even in the winter.

Denali massif, Alaska

Consumption – Take a different approach when buying clothes.

Dressing ourselves is such a commonplace action that we rarely consider the societal and environmental impacts of the clothes we buy. Who made them? How far did they have to travel before they could be sold? What are they made of? Polyester, nylon and fake fur are not biodegradable, and their manufacture from non-renewable petrochemical products uses large amounts of water and energy. Cotton uses large quantities of pesticides. Wool, linen, and hemp, on the other hand, are more environmentally friendly; also look for organic cotton.

―――――――――

Choose clothes and shoes that are manufactured in the United Kingdom or EU, with fabric made from organic crops, or that is traded fairly. Consider buying second-hand clothes from thrift stores or charity shops.

Iceberg, Greenland

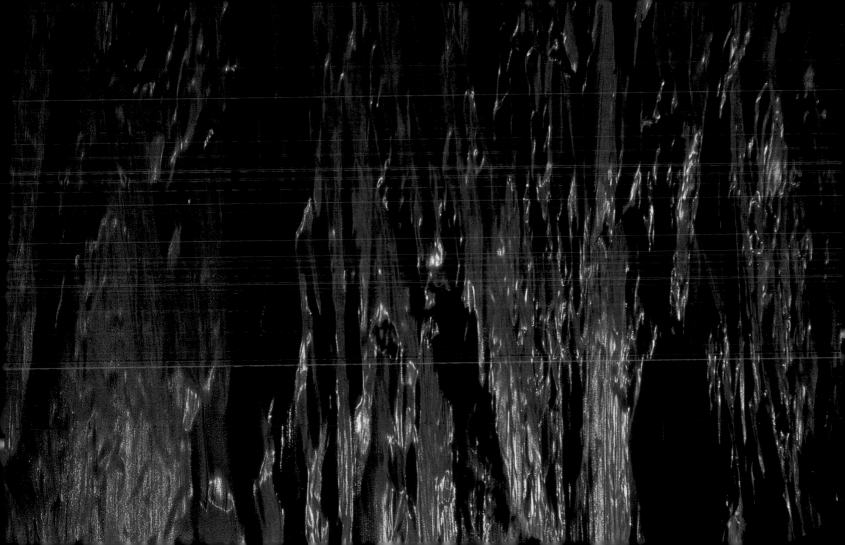

Water – Do not throw your waste into the gutter.

Globally, most domestic and industrial wastewater returns to the environment untreated. In China, 80 per cent of industrial wastewater, often loaded with toxic substances, is emptied directly into the environment, destroying fauna and flora and polluting the fresh water supply. The impact of such actions is made all the more serious by the fact that industries in developing countries often produce much more pollution than their counterparts in wealthier countries.

In cities, storm water runoff, which flows along gutters and then into storm drains, is not treated either: it flows directly into rivers. Do not throw litter or waste into the gutter: it will follow the same path as the water.

Cerro Torre, Patagonia, Argentina

Biodiversity – Don't keep exotic animals as pets.

Exotic animals have been snatched in their thousands from their natural habitats. They end up in captivity where they suffer greatly, distressed at being caged and often being taken to live in climates to which they are unsuited. The black market for exotics has devastated the populations of some unlucky species. The horned parrot of New Caledonia, for example, is highly sought after, and the victim of ferocious poaching: only 1,700 remain in the wild. In recent years, in the United Kingdom the number of exotic animals kept as pets has increased dramatically. It is perhaps the fastest growing sector in the pet market.

Think carefully before buying an iguana, python or colourful parrot. They might make an unusual pet, but in the interests of both the natural world and the animal itself, stick to the more conventional dog or cat.
www.rspca.org.uk

Marine iguana, Argentina

Waste – Watch out for the plastic rings that hold together six-pack cans.

The world's oceans are severely affected by pollution, and three-quarters of the detritus that pollutes the sea comes from the land. Every year, over 6 billion kilograms of rubbish are released into our oceans worldwide. The flexible plastic loops that connect six-packs of cans are often dropped on beaches. They seem harmless, but they are deadly once they float out to sea, where seals, dolphins, and sea birds trap their snouts, beaks, or heads in them – often with fatal results.

A study of beaches in Texas found that 70 per cent of all rubbish left behind was made of plastic, which never biodegrades. Instead, plastic photo-degrades, a process by which it breaks into ever smaller pieces, which are then consumed by fish and wildlife. So, make sure your own rubbish does not reach the sea: help reduce litter on the street or it will end up in storm drains, which eventually drain into the sea.

Nudibranche (sea slug), Australia

Waste – Choose goods with less packaging.

When we buy something, we tend to look at its quality and its price. Less attention is given to the packaging. However, packaging accounts for part of the cost of the product – sometimes a considerable part.

––––––––––––––––

Why does a tube of toothpaste have to come in a cardboard box? Why do printer cartridges come in both cardboard and plastic packaging? Why must bananas be sealed in plastic? Does this excess packaging really improve the quality of products? When you have a choice between equivalent products, choose the one with less packaging.

White Desert, Egypt

Lifestyle – Offer a skill to a local environmental organisation.

Different environmental associations use peaceful but high profile ways to make themselves heard by governments and to make the public aware of issues. Some fight spectacular media or legal campaigns, others organise animal censuses and nature walks, clean up beaches after an oil spill, or collect rubbish from beaches and rivers. All, however, need volunteers.

Support, or join, an organisation involved in the protection of the environment. If you are skilled in a particular trade, offer your services. By giving just a little of your time, you will be able to take concrete action and speak on behalf of many of your fellow citizens on environmental issues.

Iceberg, Greenland

Energy – Look for the logos and labels that identify energy-saving computer equipment.

In the United States, the Energy Star logo helps consumers to identify energy-efficient office equipment that has been manufactured according to the energy-saving recommendations in the Kyoto Protocol. The Energy Star logo appears on all computer equipment (monitors, scanners, printers) that incorporates energy-efficient features. The European Union's Eco-label was introduced in 1993 to encourage the manufacture of less environmentally damaging products and was adopted for personal computers in 1999.

Look for the Eco-label when you buy computer equipment (a flower with the blue stars of the EU flag encircling a green 'E'). The savings will benefit your electricity bill as well as the environment.

Lava, Kilauea volcano, Hawaii

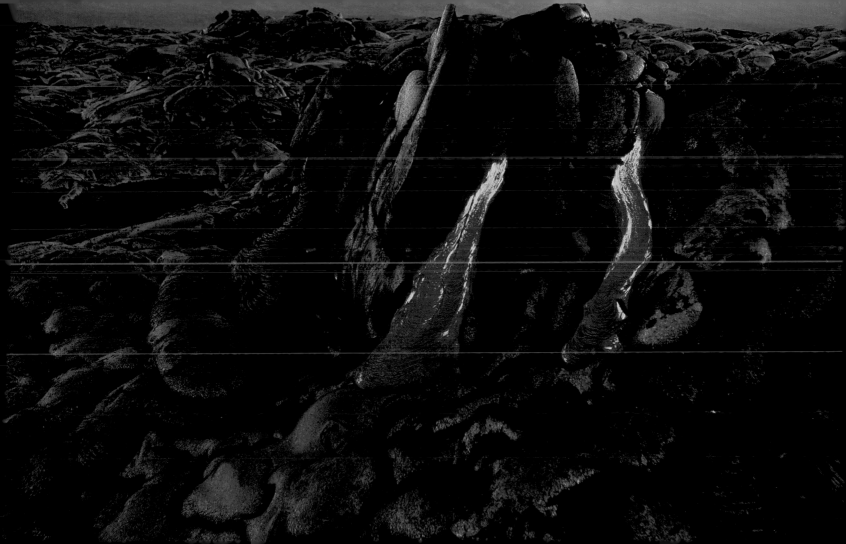

Water – Have aerators fitted.

Some 80 per cent of the world's the fresh water consumption is used for irrigating crops and generating thermoelectric-power. Worldwide, irrigated areas, which have increased by as much as 7 times over the last 100 years, use two-thirds of the water that is drawn off from rivers and aquifers. The amount of water drawn off is expected to rise by a further 14 per cent by 2020.

You can reduce your domestic consumption of water by having aerators fitted. The water flow will feel stronger, but it will actually consist of less water and more air. The flow through conventional taps is 19 to 57 litres a minute; aerated taps can reduce the amount of water used by 30 to 40 per cent.

Niagara Falls, United States

Agriculture – Do not buy foods containing genetically modified crops.

Scientists have mastered the technology that enables them to alter the genes of plants and animals, producing genetically modified (GM) crops. The resulting transgenic plants – for example, maize, cotton and soya – are immune to insects and diseases, resistant to drought, or richer in nutrients. Unfortunately, these crops are not the answer to all agriculture and food supply problems. They pose human and environmental risks, some of which are known, but many of which still remain to be discovered.

The vast majority of genetically engineered crops currently on the market have been modified either to withstand herbicide, so that more can be sprayed to combat weeds, or to produce their own insecticide. GM crops contribute to the skyrocketing levels of pesticide use in today's agricultural market. Foods containing GM crops are labeled; therefore, you can avoid buying them. Lists of manufacturers who declare their products to be GMO free can be obtained. Organic foods do not contain them.
www.smart-publications.com/articles/021015-gmo.html

Miachik volcano, Kamchatka, Russia

Transport – Change your car over to biodiesel.

Biodiesel is a clean-burning alternative to both conventional diesel and petrol, although cars with petrol engines have to be modified in order to burn it. Biodiesel is simple to use, biodegradable, non-toxic and emits far fewer emissions than conventional diesel. Biodiesel cars give off 78 per cent fewer emissions and, because it is made from vegetable and animal fat, it does not deplete the already dwindling oil supply.

As more people decide to use Biodiesel, its price will fall and the more outlets will stock it.

Sunset, Sudan

Gardening – Use natural treatments for diseases.

The intensive use of chemicals and defoliants in both agriculture and gardening impoverishes the soil, which ultimately becomes sterile. Even worse, repeated and systematic treatment with these agents encourages the development of resistance in the very pests that they are intended to kill . Since the 1950s, the number of insect and mite species immune to insecticides has increased from a dozen to nearly 450.

Rather than have to treat plant diseases, it is preferable to prevent them occurring in the first place. You can help to do this by choosing the right plants for your site, choosing disease-resistant varieties, and by keeping the garden clean, ensuring the soil is well balanced and by not over-watering.

St Helens National Monument, United States

march 22nd

Water – Do not let your children play with running water.

We take access to clean running water so much for granted that we rarely think about what life would be like without it, but for much of the world water is not on tap. Every morning, millions of people have to walk long distances to collect the water that is essential to their modest daily needs. The average African woman walks over 5 kilometres a day to obtain water for her family, which is the equivalent of a marathon course every week. March 22 has been designated World Water Day and aims to make people aware of the importance of preserving this vital resource.

Teach your children to treat water with respect. The taps in the bath and the garden hose are not playthings. Do not let your children play with running water – it is extremely wasteful.

Indian summer, Canada

Water – Run the dishwasher only when it is full.

A large proportion of the water taken from nature to meet people's growing needs is drawn off rivers. Instead of flowing into the sea, rivers such as the Colorado in the United States and Mexico, the Jordan in the Middle East, the Indus in Pakistan, the Yellow River in China and the Nile in Egypt vanish into the earth at certain times of the year in certain places, because their volume is reduced. Rivers and streams in the United States suffer the same fate because of groundwater depletion. This happens during the dry months of the summer when the baseflows of rivers are low and water is being pumped to irrigate lawns and gardens, as well as for use in homes.

Your dishwasher uses 10 to 15 litres per cycle, which is less than washing dishes by hand. To save water, only run it when it is completely full.

Guelta (water hole), Niger

march 24th

Agriculture – Avoid fast-food chains.

An astonishing 852 million people around the world are living in poverty. Of these, 815 million live in developing countries. In 1996, the governments of the countries that belong to the United Nations Food and Agriculture Organisation (FAO) made a commitment to halve the number of malnourished people in the world by 2015. At the present rate of progress this target will not be reached until 2150 – more than 100 years late.

———————————

Meanwhile, no part of the world is safe from the onslaught of fast food – chains of restaurants continue to advance across continents, carrying the flag of globalisation before them. Think twice before you visit a fast-food restaurant and if you do, make your children aware of the results of mass-produced food: intensive, polluting agriculture, poor nutritional quality, mountains of non-recyclable packaging, as well as poor nutritional quality and the standardisation of taste that comes from the lack of variety.
www.bread.org/

Vestmannaeyjar Islands, Iceland

Water – Wait till evening to water your garden.

All the water we use runs into rivers, from where it flows to the sea to evaporate and fall on to the earth once more as rain. This endless process is called the water cycle. Since the amount of water on earth is always the same, the water that quenches our thirst today may have been drunk by dinosaurs millions of years ago. It cannot be replenished other than in the natural cycle so we need to look after it.

―――――――――

Wait until evening to water your garden; during the cooler hours of the night, plants lose less through evaporation and use half as much water. Also keep the weather forecast in mind: there is no sense watering your garden if rain is in the forecast. When the dry months come, leave the lawn, it will turn brown but the grass will soon turn green again when the rain comes.

Niger River, Mali

Energy – Choose a dishwasher with a 'booster' heater and then reduce your water heater temperature.

More than a third of the electricity used by an average household goes to supply power for washing machines, dishwashers and dryers. About 80 per cent of the total energy used by dishwashers goes towards heating the water.

To reduce this consumption of energy, choose a dishwasher with a 'booster' heater. It will add a small amount to the cost of a new washer, but it should pay for itself in water-heating energy savings after about a year. Some dishwashers have boosters that will automatically raise the temperature, while others require a manual change before beginning a wash cycle.

Hot springs, Kamchatka, Russia

Lifestyle – Start a toy library.

Too many children never have the opportunity to experience a normal childhood. More than 300,000 young boys worldwide are enlisted as child soldiers. Many are not even 10 years old. A total of 352 million children aged between 5 and 17 are forced to work; more than 246 million of these illegally, and almost 171 million under dangerous conditions.

———————————

In order to teach your children that there are alternatives to buying and consuming things, set up a toy library with friends. The variety of shared toys will certainly entertain the kids, and the toys will be used by more than one child, thereby reducing the number of toys that have to be produced.

Kilauea volcano, Hawaii

Waste – Leftover and stripped paint should go to the dump.

Painting the house is a polluting business. Cans containing leftover paint, cloths, soiled packaging, solvents and glue thrown in the dustbin get mixed up with other household waste. They have a damaging effect on the decomposition of the gases produced by incineration and on the effluent from a landfill. If thrown down the drain, their toxicity interferes with the processes of water treatment plants. Half of all this waste does not get treated and thus ends up in rivers and the sea. Three-quarters of marine pollution comes from fresh water.

There are several ways to deal with or minimise the effect of painting your house: first, take careful measurements and only buy exactly the amount of paint that you need; once you have finished a project, give leftover paint to a community scheme or donate it to a local charity if they are willing to accept it. Finally, if you must dispose of the paint, be sure to let it dry fully (adding sawdust or cat litter as needed) before putting it in the dustbin.

Glacier, Greenland

Biodiversity – When on holiday, do not eat turtle meat.

Today 6 of the world's 7 species of turtle are in danger of being wiped out. Killed for their meat and shells, their eggs are also collected, their laying sites are disturbed and they are victims of pollution. In Malaysia, the number of leatherback turtle nests has dropped by 98 per cent since 1950. Around 100,000 green turtles are killed each year in the islands that lie between Australia and Malaysia, while in Indonesia their numbers are a tenth of what they were during the 1940s. The killing of young adults for their meat is all the more damaging because they do not reach sexual maturity until the age of around 25 years old.

**When you are on holiday, you will see turtle meat on the menu in some restaurants.
Eating it encourages a trade that threatens to wipe out a species that has been protected internationally since 1990.**

Leatherback turtle, Guyana

Water – Take a shower rather than a bath.

More than a third of humanity lacks adequate sanitation. It is estimated that patients suffering from preventable, water-borne diseases occupy half the world's hospital beds. In 2004, the World Health Organisation estimated that more than 2.6 billion people – 40 per cent of the world's population – do not have access to basic sanitation and more than one billion people use unsafe sources of drinking water. This lack of access to clean water kills 4,000 children every day.

Do not take for granted what the rest of the world sorely needs. Moderate your water use – start by taking shorter showers. A shower lasting 5 minutes uses 25 to 80 litres, while a full bath requires 200 to 250 litres of water.

Glacier National Park, United States

Air – Have your car's pollution emissions checked.

All new petrol and diesel cars are fitted with a catalytic converter, which cuts noise and treats the car's exhaust gases before they are released into the atmosphere, significantly reducing the pollutants. However, since the increase in the number of vehicles on roads worldwide is overwhelming, this is not enough to stop pollution. There are 800 million cars and lorries on the road today; by 2050, if present trends continue, there will be 2 billion.

It is essential, therefore, to have your car's exhaust emissions checked regularly. Think about whether you absolutely need to buy that new car or not. If you live in a town or city, perhaps you could use public transport for the majority of your journeys, using your old car only when necessary (but do keep an eye on those emission levels). Or consider car sharing with a friend or colleague. This will reduce the number of times you use the car on a daily basis and corresponding wear and tear.

Red ibis, Brazil

Agriculture – Buy more Fair Trade products.

Fair Trade accounts for not even one per cent of world trade. It directly benefits some 800,000 producers and their families (more than 5 million people in around 50 countries) and allows them to meet their needs for food, health, housing, education and social security. However, the broadening of the Fair Trade market to embrace new co-operatives in developing countries depends on demand, which in turn depends on the awareness of consumers in Europe, the United States and Japan.

In the UK, consumers spent over £140 million on Fair Trade-marked products in 2004, an increase of 51 per cent over the previous year. Coffee accounts for 35 per cent of the total. But don't stop at Fair Trade coffee. Why not include other Fair Trade products in your shopping basket: choose from tea, chocolate, orange juice, bananas, pineapples, rice, honey, sugar and many more.

Yellowstone River Canyon, United States

Lifestyle – Act now to preserve the environment. Make the first move, do not wait for someone else to do it.

It is easy to say to yourself that one small polluting or harmful action will not endanger the earth's future. However, when these small actions are repeated across the world, they build up to create problems of dramatic proportions. Similarly, one small, isolated action to preserve the environment will not improve matters on its own, but if these actions are repeated every day by millions of people, they will have a significant effect. If the majority adopt environmental practices as a new way of life, they will contribute to preserving the earth and its riches for future generations.

Do not wait for friends or neighbours to set an example. Make the first move yourself. They might be waiting for you!

Icebergs, Greenland

Chemicals – Use biodegradable cleaning products.

In the local supermarket we can buy acids, phenols, oil derivatives, corrosive solutions, chlorine and an entire arsenal of toxic products, all supposedly necessary for keeping our homes clean... if we are to believe the adverts.

—————

Choose environmentally friendly and biodegradable household cleaning products that do not contain the most dangerous substances. You will be contributing to the preservation of the soil, air and water.

Giant clam, Australia

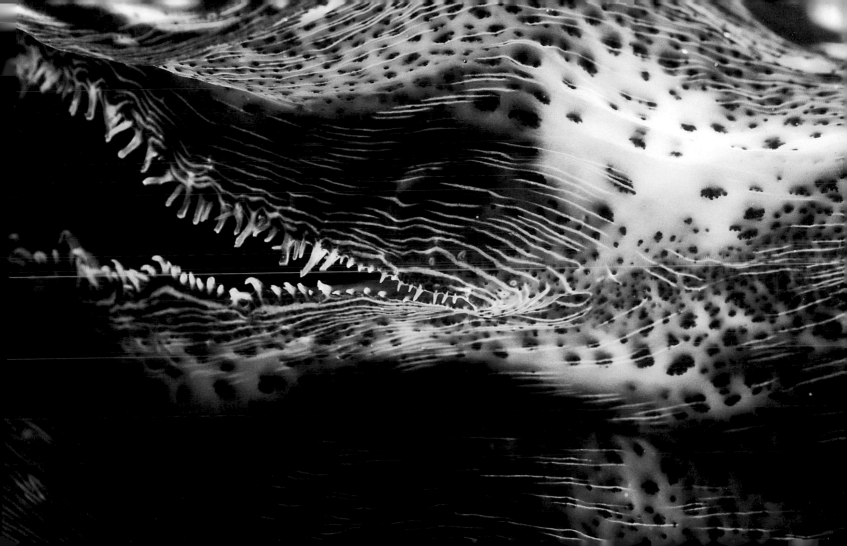

Transport – Try an electric bike.

Preserving the quality of the air around us is vital to life and our well-being. Air pollution kills 3 times as many people as road accidents. It causes respiratory diseases (chronic bronchitis, asthma, sinusitis) and is responsible for 3 million deaths worldwide every year.

Why not try an electric bicycle. It is an attractive alternative to the car for short journeys. The electric motor saves your legs by halving the effort needed to pedal, and it includes a removable, easily rechargeable battery. However, most importantly, it emits no pollution and is silent, and you can leave the cars behind in a traffic jam.

Uzon caldera, Kamchatka, Russia

Agriculture – Buy traditional varieties of fruit and vegetables.

In its headlong rush for profitability, the agricultural industry has favoured the most productive and disease-resistant types of produce at the expense of many native varieties of fruit and vegetables that are regarded as less desirable. It has been established that around 80 per cent of tomato and 92 per cent of lettuce varieties have been lost. Some of these, neglected for decades, survive only in special conservation facilities.

Standardisation is gaining ground at the expense of biological diversity. Think about varying your choice of fruit and vegetables; try different types and rediscover traditional varieties. Local farms often revive seed stock and sometimes develop their own delicious types of produce based on historical varieties.

Cranberries, United States

Biodiversity – Leave protected plants and animals alone.

Every hour, more than 2 species of plant or animal disappear from the earth. In the space of just a century, more than 100 species of mammal and 150 bird species have been wiped out for good. The chief causes of biodiversity loss are the destruction of natural habitats, the introduction of foreign species and the excessive exploitation of species. Some especially threatened species are now protected: whales, turtles, rhinoceroses, tigers, pandas and orchids are among the best known. However, there are thousands of other less well known but equally significant species.

When you visit wild places, do not destroy or remove protected plant or animal species. Instead, find out more about them and discover how you can contribute to their protection and restoration.

Albatross, Roaring Forties, off the coast of South Africa

Chemicals – Wash your windows with vinegar.

Most of the world's pollution comes from developed countries, which produce more than 95 per cent of dangerous pollution. However, in these countries the regulations governing the disposal of dangerous industrial waste have become so strict and involve so much expense that companies have turned to developing countries to take their waste. And industry is not the only area in which chemical products proliferate.

Most window cleaning fluids contain synthetic compounds that are harmful to rivers. Replace them with a bucket of water, to which you have added a few spoonfuls of vinegar. Apply this with a cloth or newspaper, rather than with a paper towel.

Bacteria, Kamchatka, Russia

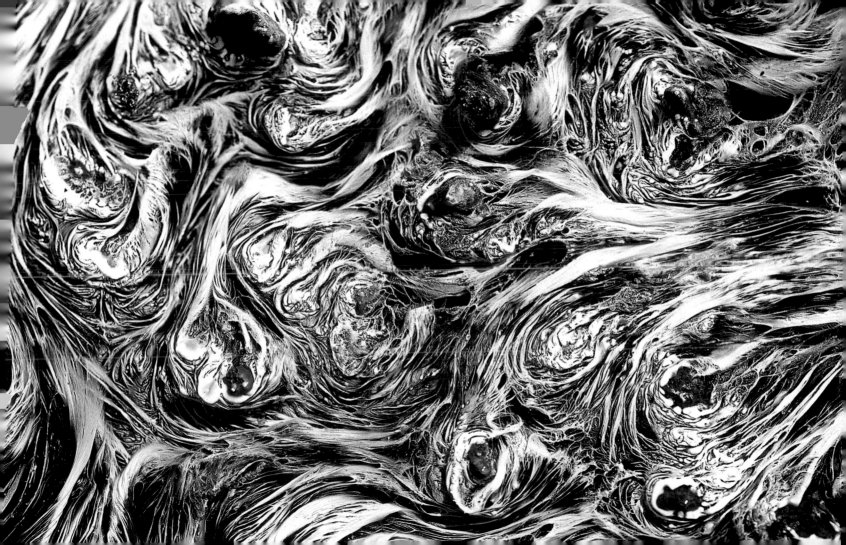

Lifestyle – Lobby your MP about the environment – make your feelings known.

If you feel that your local authority should adopt the LEED (Leadership in Energy and Environmental Design) standard for new buildings and use more renewable energy, if you think that energy is used wastefully in public buildings and street lighting, or if you disagree with your area's transport and development plans, make your feelings known.

Lobby your MP to make him (or her) listen to your environmental concerns and urge them to take decisions that fit with sustainable development. The democratic process needs input from the people, and remember, your elected officials represent you!

Mount Fitz Roy, Argentina

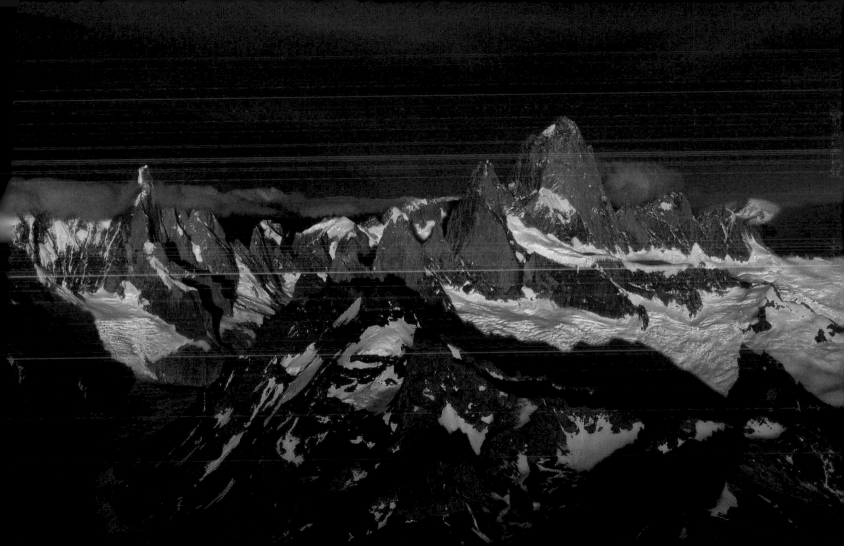

Waste – When you eat out, eat in.

In the space of about 30 years the volume of waste generated by household packaging has risen by 5 times, and by as much as 50 times in the case of certain materials such as plastic. During the 1970s, the appearance of containers made of PVC (polyvinyl chloride) allowed the manufacture of 'disposable' items, to be thrown out after a single use. The trend towards the use of such items has intensified, and is now closely connected to the recent fashion among consumers for eating on the move.

At work, when taking your lunch hour, avoid buying take-away meals, which produce large quantities of waste, especially non-recyclable plastic. Take the time to sit down and enjoy your food on the premises.

Scorpion fish, Thailand

Agriculture – Buy organic food for your baby.

Studies have shown that human exposure to pesticides can cause neurological disturbances, increase the frequency of certain cancers, damage the immune system and reduce male fertility. Pesticides degrade soil and contaminate drinking water, leading to significant clean-up costs. These chemicals also kill non-targeted insects and affect all organisms higher up in the food chain. A conventional farmer might use as many as 450 different authorised pesticides, whereas an organic farmer might use just 7 natural pesticides, and only then in a controlled way.

─────────

If 'going organic' for the whole family looks like a daunting project, at least give priority to feeding organic foods to babies and young children. The average child has 4 times more exposure than an adult to at least 10 widely used cancer-causing pesticides. Pesticides can increase susceptibility to certain cancers by breaking down the immune system's resistance to cancer cells. Infants and children are among those at greatest risk.
www.soilassociation.org/

White Desert, Egypt

Transport – Cycle or walk for short trips.

We cheerfully use the car to travel short distances. A national survey showed that the average annual distance travelled in a car has increased. In the lowest income bracket, drivers typically travel less than 8 kilometres on average in their motor vehicles. In the highest income bracket, drivers average twice that per trip.

———————————

Choose to cycle or walk instead. A walk of just one kilometre, or just over half a mile, into town takes less than 15 minutes! It is difficult to beat that in a car, when you think of the time spent looking for somewhere to park. You will save fuel and the world will be spared yet more greenhouse gas emissions and climatic upheaval.

Salar de Uyuni, Bolivia

april 12th

Gardening – Prevent soil erosion.

Soil erosion is caused by wind and rain and is aggravated by human activity. The texture of the soil, the gradient of the ground and the plants growing in it all play a part. When soil becomes impacted through heavy rainfall, water is not able to penetrate the surface and so runs off, eroding the edges of riverbanks and ponds as it does so. Bare spots on a lawn and exposed shrub and tree roots are signs of soil erosion in a garden. Signs of erosion in the countryside are muddy water in streams or drainage ditches, the build-up of silt and the widening and deepening of streams and rivers.

Help prevent soil erosion: use mulch on flower beds, install guttering and downpipes that discharge rain water onto areas where it won't cause damage, and protect the soil where it enters the ground by using splash blocks or drainage tiles.

Seeds, Shenandoah National Park, United States

Water – Do not waste water when travelling to places where it is scarce.

About 65 per cent of the water people use is pumped from underground aquifers. However, more is drawn off than is naturally replaced because impervious surfaces such as pavement and buildings prevent rainwater from entering the ground; therefore, aquifers are gradually being drained dry. Some aquifers close to the sea – in Spain, for example – have started to fill up with salt water. In India, the water table has dropped by between up to 3 metres over three-quarters of the country's area. This shortage is evidence of the need for proper conservation and management instead of technological fixes, such as desalinisation plants, to access more water.

_____

In some countries, water is scarce. Think about it when you are travelling. In developing countries, the average tourist uses as much water in 24 hours as a local villager does in 100 days. Be careful: take as few baths as possible and avoid wasting this precious liquid.

Namib Desert, Namibia

Biodiversity – Refuse to buy any objects made from ivory.

Massacred for the ivory of its tusks, the numbers of African elephant are now dwindling massively. In Kenya and Tanzania, about 70,000 African elephants were killed each year between 1975 and 1980. Between 1980 and 2000, their numbers fell from 1.4 million to 400,000.

Although the international ivory trade was banned in 1990, jewellery and statuettes made from ivory can still be bought in African and Asian markets. If traders offer you ivory objects illegally, do not buy them. It encourages trafficking and, since the trade in ivory items is illegal, you will not be allowed to take them home.

Elephant, Kenya

Agriculture – Choose a well-bred chicken.

By breeding fowl using growth-promoting drugs and antibiotics, farmers have succeeded in decreasing the average amount of time it takes to produce an average 2.2 kilogram chicken, from 84 days in 1950 to 50 days today. Living conditions for these battery-raised animals are crowded and grim; these birds never even see the light of day. Recently, free-range and organically-raised chicken has become more widely available as an alternative, although organic farmers in the UK may keep flocks of up to 12,000 birds, in line with European Union standards. Instead, seek out organic and free-range chickens and eggs marked with the more stringent Soil Association label. These animals live in flocks of no more than 2,000 and ideally no bigger than 500 birds. Their diet includes organic grain, but no drugs. While more expensive to produce, humanely raised chickens are healthier and they taste better.

Consider reducing your meat consumption and replace quantity with quality. Think about how that inexpensive, intensively raised roast came to market and treat yourself to the somewhat more costly, but much happier, organic bird. Choose meat, dairy products and eggs bearing the Soil Association, IOFGA, or Organic Farmers and Growers mark.
ww.irishorganic.ie/
www.organicfarmers.uk.com/

Drifting ice floe, Antarctica

Biodiversity – Be unobtrusive while out in the countryside.

More than one-third of Europe's bird species are threatened with extinction. Birds are vulnerable to habitat damage from intensive agriculture and forestry, the growing impact of development on the land, unrestricted water use and all kinds of pollution.

When you are out in the countryside, treat wildlife with respect. Do not disturb animals, especially young animals and chicks. Watch them discreetly, from a distance, without disturbing the peace and tranquillity of their nesting places.

Primary tropical forest, Australia

Water – Trace leaks.

Worldwide, on average half the water in distribution grids and in cities is lost to leakage. Thus, the volume of water lost in Nairobi to leaks and illegal siphoning could meet the needs of Mombassa, the country's second-largest city.

Trace the leaks in your house's plumbing: a dripping tap can lose 15 litres of water a day if it drips at a rate of one drop every second. A leaking toilet can lose 45 litres a day.

Mud flats, Alaska

Agriculture – Count your calories – production calories, that is.

Every product you purchase has two calorific values – one value for the amount of energy you receive from it (the value printed on the side of the package) and one for the amount of energy it takes to produce the food. In today's industrial food system, these energy inputs come from a variety of sources: the sun, the energy used by the people who make or prepare the product, and fossil fuel sources that drive the machinery used in the farming process and power the production of chemicals. Some of the statistics are hard to take on board: modern production and distribution systems use up 10 to 15 calories of energy for every calorie of food energy produced; the USA uses 3 times more energy per person just making and preparing food than developing countries use per person for all activity requiring energy.

A kilogram of flour requires fewer than 500 kilocalories (k cal) of energy to process it; the same amount of soda requires over 1,400 k cal; to produce chocolate requires over 18,500 k cal. To reduce the amount of energy it takes to prepare your food, try to buy as few processed foods as possible. Stick to bulk ingredients as well, to minimise energy costs for packaging, and organic foods to minimise the energy used for creating pesticides and herbicides.

Salt lakes, Chad

Natural disasters – Do not build in high-risk areas – check with your local authority.

There is a clear correlation between the impact of a natural disaster and the level of development of the country in which it takes place. Natural disasters cause 47 times more deaths in poor countries than in wealthy ones. Lacking the appropriate infrastructure and proper protection measures, developing countries are more vulnerable, especially to extremes of weather. Contributing to this problem is the fact that in the large cities of developing countries, 45 per cent of the population live in dwellings without building permits.

To reduce the social and economic costs of natural disasters, consider where you build and how you build. Proper adherence to building codes is necessary to create a more resilient and safer environment.

Erta Ale volcano, Ethiopia

Gardening – Find alternatives to peat-based compost.

According to the World Wildlife Federation, around 2,000 hectares of bog, an area 20 times the size of Monaco, is destroyed in the Republic of Ireland annually to supply peat for horticultural use in the United Kingdom, 66 per cent of which is sold to amateur gardeners. The peat is used as compost for the cultivation of flowers and vegetables while the bogs in which it originated are left barren.

Avoid using peat-based garden products. Recycle your waste and build a compost heap instead.

Lobelia, Uganda

Leisure – Become an environmental volunteer.

Sadly, the possibilities for being a volunteer environmental worker are endless, from guarding turtles laying their eggs on Mayotte, a small island off Madagascar, helping protect wolves in Romania, iguanas in Honduras, or griffon vultures in Israel, to assisting scientists in the conservation of endangered primates in Kenya. By volunteering for this kind of work, you can really get to know a country, immersing yourself in the local culture, while working to protect its animal and plant life at the same time.

If you want to spend your next holiday doing something both unusual and useful, think about volunteering for nature conservation; it will give you the opportunity to work with specialists and to do something positive in support of a major ecological cause.

Scorpion fish, Australia

Lifestyle – Celebrate Earth Day and do something positive for the environment.

In 1998, 25 million environmental refugees had to flee from the ravaging effects of desertification, deforestation, industrial accidents and natural disasters. This figure surpassed the 23 million who became refugees due to war. As a result of climate change, environmental refugees will become increasingly numerous, driven from their homes by drought, floods, extremes of weather and rising sea levels. It is estimated that by 2020, 20 million people will have been forced to leave Bangladesh, a vast delta on the Indian sub-continent that is especially vulnerable to being swamped. Where will they go?

Every year, on April 22, more than 180 countries celebrate Earth Day. Join the party and take part in the events organised on that day. But why stop there? Be environmentally aware and make every day Earth Day.

Salar de Uyuni, Bolivia

april 23rd

Consumption – Try trading skills instead of purchasing services.

People all around you have a wealth of talent and knowledge that perhaps you do not. Likewise, you can offer them your skills. These can be professional – computer programming, financial investment, portrait photography – or more basic, such as lifting boxes or feeding a cat while the owner is away. Instead of looking in the phone book to hire a service, contact your neighbours and friends and offer them a trade. It is another way of encouraging the world to move towards a more humane form of society.

———————————

Perhaps someone living near you will offer the help you need in moving home, in exchange for help with child minding.

Waimea Canyon, Hawaii

april 24th

Gardening – Choose compost and natural fertilisers rather than chemical fertilisers.

Excessive use of chemical fertilisers containing nitrogen contributes to pollution of water by nitrates. Highly soluble, these chemicals are easily washed away by rain and carried into rivers and aquifers. Nitrates contribute to the eutrophication of rivers, causing them to become over-rich in nutrients, so that algae grow rapidly and deplete the oxygen supply, suffocating any life forms in the water. In groundwater, large amounts of nitrates interfere with drinking water supplies.

Use natural fertilisers in your garden – stone meal, bone meal, or wood ash – and compost made from organic waste to improve soil structure and fertility in a natural and effective way that is also sustainable.

Moss, Kamchatka, Russia

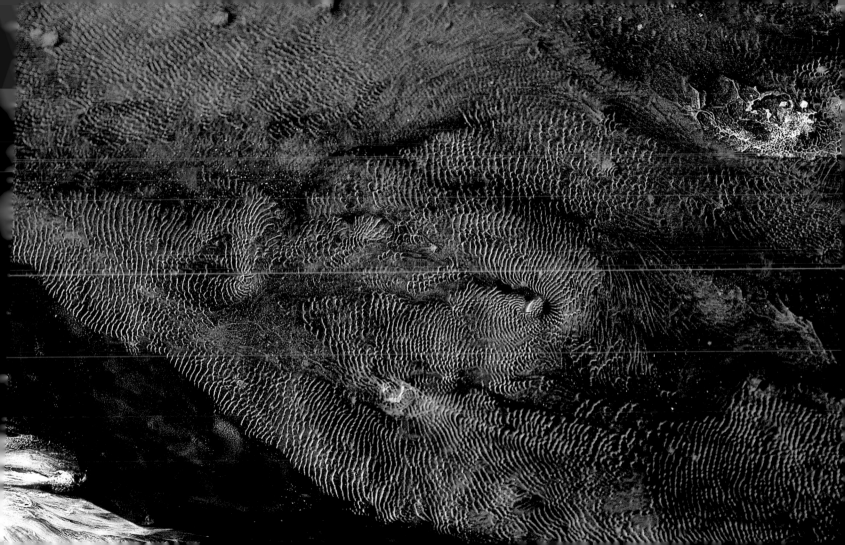

Water – Protect rivers: Don't dump or litter in storm drains.

No fewer than 114 great rivers, or half the world's biggest watercourses, are severely polluted. The Ganges, sacred though it is for Indians, is polluted by 1,137 million litres of wastewater every day, transforming it into a vast open sewer. Worldwide, 2 million tonnes of waste are poured into lakes and rivers every day. As a result, a fifth of the earth's 10,000 species of freshwater fish are in danger of extinction.

———————————

Protect rivers from all pollution. Don't dump into storm drains, which discharge into water bodies without any filtration or treatment. Also, do not drop any rubbish in the street or countryside. Sooner or later, it will inevitably be washed into a river, lake or harbour.

Guelta (water hole), Chad

Energy – Cool off without resorting to air conditioning.

Despite its environmental impact – namely, the creation of hundreds of thousands of tonnes of cancer-causing radioactive waste – nuclear power is still considered a reasonable energy-producing option, because it emits no carbon dioxide. This is undeniably a plus in trying to limit global warming, however, it does not solve the problem of the 200,000 tonnes of nuclear waste now stored across the world, 5 per cent of which will remain dangerous for several thousand years to come. Using less power, however, reduces the amount of nuclear waste produced.

Carefully consider your options before installing air conditioning: it can increase your electricity bill by a third. A fan uses one-tenth of the energy used by an air conditioning system; sunshades, blinds, shutters, and the cool of the night use no energy at all.

Iceberg, Greenland

Forests – Choose FSC-certified products.

In 1997, the Brazilian government admitted that 80 per cent of the wood taken from the tropical rainforest was removed illegally. A World Bank report declared that 80 per cent of Indonesia's wood products were also illegal. By buying Forest Stewardship Council (FSC)-certified wood, you can be sure that it comes from a sustainably managed forest where strict environmental, social and economic standards are observed, and that it does not contribute to the worldwide plundering of the tropical rainforest.

It is up to us as consumers to help increase the area of certified forest by asking for products bearing the FSC label. Currently, it appears on about 10,000 products (furniture, floor tiles, shelves, paper, garden furniture and barbecue charcoal), so make sure you take advantage of it.

Mangroves, Australia

Construction – Use photovoltaic (PV) panels to produce electricity for the home.

Solar energy is available everywhere and is free. You do not have to live in a hot, sunny country in order to take advantage of it. Fit photovoltaic (solar electric) panels to the roof of your house. They generate electricity from sunlight and are usually designed to charge 12-volt batteries. PV panels are completely silent and operate without producing any kind of pollution or dangerous waste matter.

It is usually possible to obtain a government grant towards the cost of installation and if you produce more electricity than you need, you might be able to sell the excess back to the national grid.

Antarctic peninsula

Water – Have a dual-flush fixture fitted to your toilet.

All our buildings are supplied with drinking water, water that has been treated to make sure that it is fit for human consumption, yet only one per cent of this water is actually drunk. A dual-flush toilet fixture can reduce the amount of drinking water that is used in activities that do not require water of this standard. It senses the contents of the toilet bowl and uses an appropriate amount of water to flush.

Have a dual-flush fixture fitted to your toilet, it will allow you to halve your water consumption when flushing the toilet.

Lake Turkana, Kenya

Agriculture – Demand organic products in the workplace and in schools.

Every year, about 3 million people around the world are poisoned and 200,000 die from pesticide use. In fact, pesticides are between 10 and 100 times more toxic than they were in the 1970s. A common way that they affect human health is through the chemicals seeping into the drinking water supply. Since it takes several centuries for groundwater supplies (the major source of our drinking water) to be replaced, this contamination poses a grave threat. Less polluting agricultural methods will help safeguard the future of our drinking water.

————————

Organic food has a place in institutions and companies: encourage your child's school, or the canteen at your workplace, to buy organic and locally grown products.
www.toxicslink.org

Piton de la Fournaise volcano, Réunion

Waste – Do not throw out your children's old toys.

The unchecked consumption of the world's natural resources and growing mountain of waste are largely due to the actions of the United States, Europe and Japan, where 20 per cent of the world's population live. An American household produces over 650 kilograms of household rubbish per year, which is about twice as much as a European household and 10 times as much as one in a developing country. During their lifetime, children born in industrialised countries will consume more resources and generate more pollution than 40 children in a developing country.

When your child grows out of a toy, encourage him or her to donate it to charity or to a children's hospital, and explain the benefits of doing this.

Weddell seal, Antarctica

Agriculture – Join an organic vegetable box delivery scheme.

In the UK, food now travels from farm to table 50 per cent further than it did 20 years ago, leaving in its wake a host of negative environmental and societal effects. Unable to compete with large-scale producers, rural farmers are being forced out of business. Exhaust emissions from transporting the food contribute to our pollution-laden atmosphere, while the food shipping industry relies heavily on the abundance of cheap energy sources. At the far end of this food chain, the consumer rarely knows from which hemisphere his or her banana has arrived, let alone what it took to produce it.

Community Supported Agriculture (CSA) programmes seek to alleviate these problems by localising food production and consumption. Consumers can participate by signing up for weekly deliveries of locally grown, seasonal organic vegetables. These 'box schemes' can be found all around the UK. Organic farming accounts for just 4 per cent of the cultivated land in the UK; the more consumers demand organic food, the more organic farming will increase with myriad benefits.
www.organicfood.co.uk/
www.whyorganic.org/

Erg (sand desert), Algeria

Gardening – Mulch soil to protect it from water evaporation and weed growth.

When weeds appear in the garden, there is a strong temptation to kill them using an environmentally damaging chemical treatment. It is better to prevent them from growing in the first place by using a natural mulch (soil covering), which also helps to retain moisture within the soil. Kept free of weeds and protected from drying out excessively, the soil will be healthier.

The soil around the base of plants, trees and bushes can be covered by using a mulch made of hay, dried grass cuttings, leaves, wood shavings, chippings, or cocoa bean shells. As well as helping to keep it moist, mulching will also help protect the soil from the erosive action of the wind.

Acid lake, Vanuatu

Energy – Invest in a tankless water heater.

Fossil fuels are substances extracted from the earth's crust and burned to produce heat or energy. These reserves are finite: at current rates of use, oil will be exhausted in about 50 years, gas in about 80 and coal in 300 years. It took millions of years for these deposits to form; 2 centuries will have been enough to exhaust them.

A gas boiler that heats water when required is better than an electric one, which operates continuously. A tankless (on demand) water heater only burns gas when you need water, and can also save as much as 50 per cent of the cost of heating water.

Trou de Fer, Réunion

Waste – Use concentrated cleaning products.

Packaging has gone beyond its original function of protecting a product and informing the consumer about its qualities or operation, to become a marketing tool. Over-packaged goods vie with each other to seduce and convince potential buyers at first glance, so that a product that was not on the shopping list ends up in the shopping basket.

————————

When buying washing machine or dishwasher powder, ignore individually packed, boxed tablets and instead choose less polluting and easily carried alternatives, such as refillable packages and, especially, concentrated liquids. Dishwashing detergent in tablet form is also higher in phosphorus, which disrupts ecosystems when released into our waterways.

Continental ice sheet, Greenland

Biodiversity – Contribute to enhancing the biodiversity in your area.

Data collected around the UK indicates that 71 per cent of butterfly species and 54 per cent of bird species have declined over the last 20 years, while in the past 40 years, 28 per cent of native plant species have dwindled. The reasons why we are losing plant, animal and insect life at such a fast rate include habitat destruction, pollution and the use of fertilisers and fossil fuels (diesel and petrol) in our cars.

Threatened and endangered species can be found in all kinds of ecosystems throughout the UK. Find out what kinds of species are listed in your area and commit to assisting in the preservation of their habitat.

Osprey Reef, Australia

Waste – Recycle your glass.

Making new glass products from recycled glass saves 80 per cent of the raw materials and 30 per cent of the energy used to make glass from scratch. The energy is saved because crushed glass melts at a lower temperature than the raw materials used for glass. In the United States, just over a quarter of all the glass made today is recycled. Compare that to Europe, where half of all glass is recycled. In England, 600,000 tonnes of glass recycled in one year saved as much energy as the whole country's primary schools use in a year.

—————

Glass can be recycled indefinitely. Keep your glass in the production stream!

Ol Donyo Lengai volcano, Tanzania

Consumption – Choose natural cosmetics, labelled with the Leaping Bunny Logo.

Many companies claim to be cruelty-free in the production of their goods, but without independent monitoring, many companies violate consumer trust: some companies contract out their animal-testing work so that they can claim that they don't test on animals; others test the ingredients separately on animals and then claim that the product is animal-testing free. The Humane Cosmetics Standard (HCS) and the Humane Household Products Standard (HHPS) have been created to help end the confusion. These are the only internationally recognised accreditations that allow consumers to easily identify and purchase cosmetic and cleaning products not tested on animals and containing no animal ingredients or byproducts. These cruelty-free products are easily identifiable by the international logo: a leaping bunny. In the UK, the standards are run by the British Union for the Abolition of Vivisection (BUAV); in America by the Coalition for Consumer Information on Cosmetics (CCIC). Without the Leaping Bunny certification, there is no way you can know what a company's practices are without contacting them directly to learn what the claim on a label means.

Don't be fooled by claims of apparent cruelty-free production.
www.buav.org

Lake Natron, Tanzania

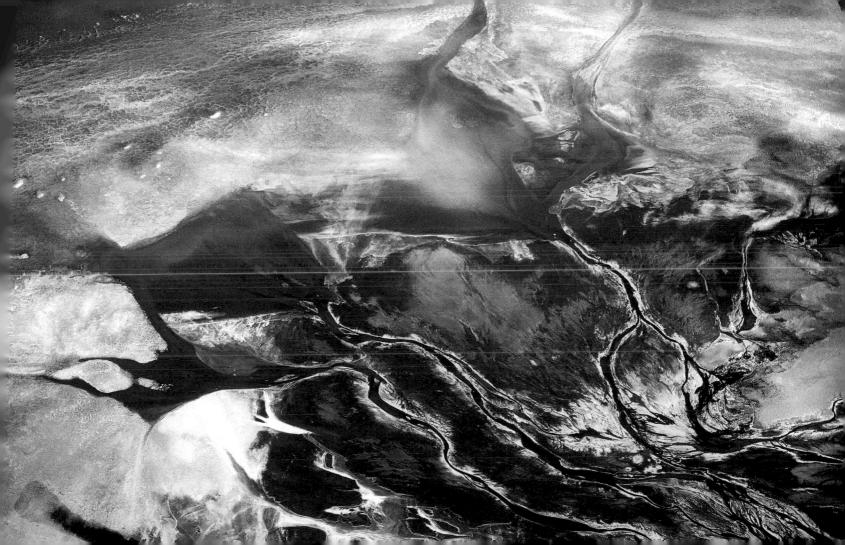

Consumption – Buy things that are durable and that can be repaired.

Every manufactured product requires raw materials and energy drawn from the environment, often out of proportion to its worth. If developed countries keep up their present rates of consumption, each individual will consume an average of 100 tonnes of the earth's non-renewable resources and more than 500 tonnes of fresh water per year (30 to 50 times as much as is available for each person in the poorest countries). Buying durable goods that can be repaired will help reduce the impact of this.

The next time you buy something, ask the seller how long the product is guaranteed, how easily it can be repaired and whether spare parts are available.

Glacial corridor, Greenland

Transport – Drive smoothly.

Today, the world burns as much oil in 6 weeks as it did in a year in 1950. Oil reserves are running out and, at current rates of consumption, they will be exhausted in about 50 years. Transport alone accounts for half the world's oil consumption.

You can help to preserve global reserves. In town, try to drive smoothly; avoid accelerating and braking too hard and too frequently. This sort of aggressive driving increases fuel consumption by 40 per cent, which means you are spending more on petrol and are contributing to urban air pollution.

Volcanic ash, Iceland

Gardening – Save ash and eggshells to discourage slugs.

Getting rid of unwanted visitors to the garden does not necessarily require chemicals. Home-made methods sometimes work much better, are easier on the pocket and cause absolutely no damage to the natural environment.

Wage war on slugs and snails the eco-friendly way and drive them away by spreading ash or crushed eggshells around the plants you wish to protect or, alternatively, plant herbs. Slugs have a particular dislike of pungent aromatic plants. You can also lay planks alongside your flowerbeds. Slugs sheltering from the sun will collect on the underside. Just turn the planks over regularly to collect the slugs and destroy them.

Cactus, Bolivia

Biodiversity – Visit regional nature reserves and parks.

Britain's countryside has an extremely rich natural heritage. National parks, forests, nature reserves and historic sites offer an insight into both the natural and cultural histories of local regions. The diversity of the landscape, breathtaking views and the richness of flora and fauna to be found in our national parks might inspire wonder and awe, but it is the commonplace, the natural world around us with which we live every day, and its long heritage, that tells us who we are.

———————

Pay a visit to a national park, forest, or reserve in your area. Learn about the species that inhabit it and any new developments that might threaten it.

Massif Central, France

Waste – Give your clothes a second life.

Fashions change, and unworn clothes gradually accumulate in wardrobes. If they are in good condition, they can be sold second-hand or given to charities. The second-hand market offers an economic, environmentally friendly alternative to new clothes. On average, the manufacture of 1,000 items of clothing produces about 225 kilograms of waste, consisting of cloth, paper and packaging.

Get rid of the clutter in your wardrobe and sort through your clothes to see which could still be put to good use. If you cannot find a suitable charitable organisation ready to take them, ask your local authority about clothing collections. And remember, as well as giving your old or unfashionable clothes to be sold second-hand, you could also shop in second-hand stores yourself.

Volcanic cone, Indonesia

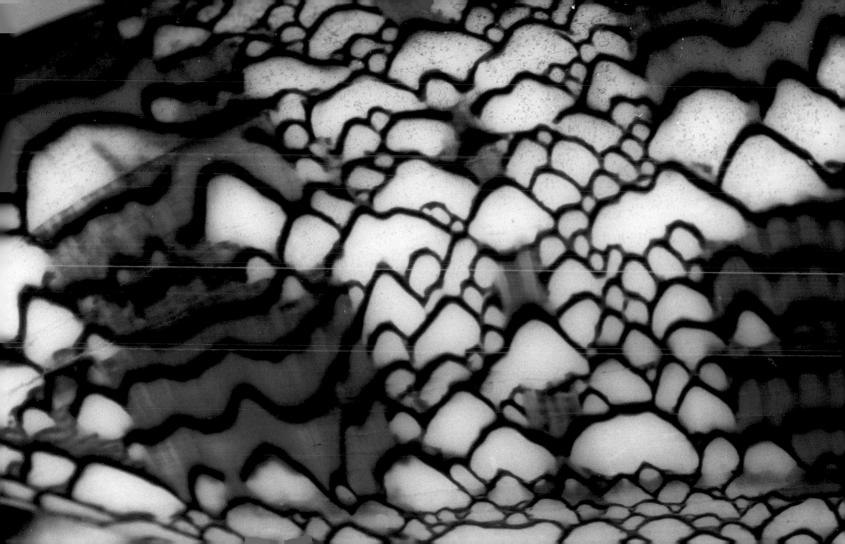

Construction – Urge your mayor and local council to assess the environmental impact of existing municipal buildings.

Britain's Building Research Establishment Environmental Assessment Method (BREEAM) addresses the environmental impact of new and existing buildings. Various problem areas are analysed, including air and noise pollution, hazardous materials, lighting and a building's impact on ozone depletion. Based on a similar premise as the EcoHomes standards for new housing construction, BREEAM also examines energy savings, water savings and healthier indoor environments.

Encourage your local council to adopt BREEAM standards for new buildings, saving your town environmentally and economically in the long term.

Lake Magadi, Kenya

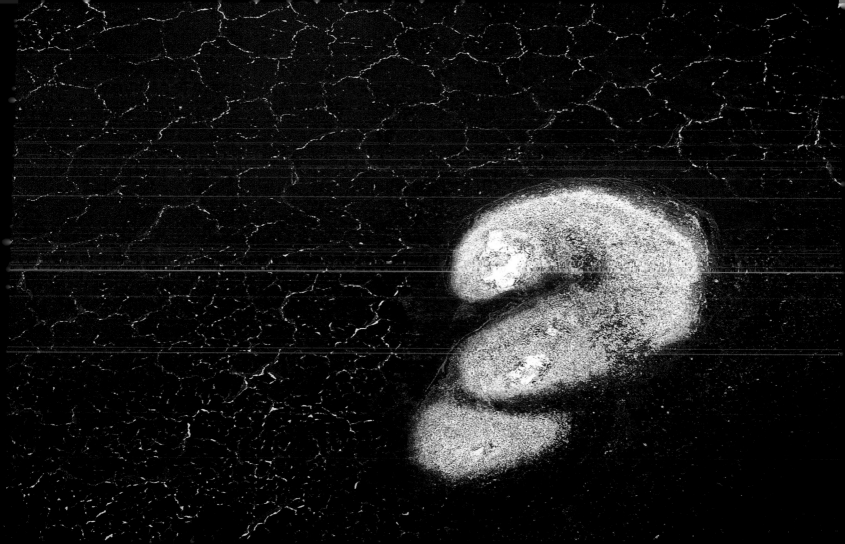

may 15th

Waste – Do not print out your emails.

Paper and card, which are both recyclable, make up 80 per cent of office waste. Despite the introduction of the 'paperless office' concept, workplaces continue an upwards trend in paper use. Between 1995 and 2000, use of copy paper increased by 30 per cent.

———————

To reduce this wasteful consumption, do not automatically print out the emails you receive. Organise your computer to file your email electronically, and only print out emails when it is essential. The average office worker uses 10,000 sheets of paper a year – help lower this statistic!

Stream, Greenland

Biodiversity – Respect the environment when horse riding.

Nature provides for us with an apparently endless bounty of food and resources: clean air to breathe, a favourable climate, an immense variety of food, fresh water (which is purified naturally), the base ingredients of medicines (with doubtless many more still to be discovered), energy resources, natural plant pollination by insects and animals (notably a third of the plants we use for food) and much more besides. Our dependence upon the natural world should encourage us to show it greater respect – our future depends on it.

Horseback riding is a environmentally friendly way of seeing the countryside: the odour of the horse masks your own scent, allowing you to approach other animals without frightening them away. But when on horseback, remember to keep to the marked trails.

Tassili du Hoggar, Algeria

Consumption – Don't discard the carpeting in your home just because you're tired of the colour.

More than 2 million tonnes of carpet materials end up in American landfill sites every year and 1.6 million tonnes of carpet waste are produced yearly in Western Europe. A great majority – up to 70 per cent – of carpeting is replaced for reasons other than wear. Replacing carpet is not only an economically expensive proposition, but an environmentally costly one as well.

Find a service that will re-dye your carpet without replacing it, or can restore your carpet to its original quality.
www.wasteonline.org.uk/resources/Wasteguide/mn_wastetypes_textiles.html

Tiger shark, Australia

Transport – Buy fruit and vegetables from your local market.

Three quarters of the edible fruit and vegetable varieties that were cultivated at the beginning of the 20th century have since disappeared. Today's varieties, which have survived the race to increase productivity, are mostly hybrids, chosen for their ability to withstand the various demands of mechanised farming and produce distribution. Picked while still unripe and ripened artificially, once on the shelf they look almost perfect, but are hiding a general lack of flavour and nutritional value.

Buy your fruit and vegetables from the market or shops that stock local produce. You will be supporting the local economy, and your purchases will be more environmentally friendly since they involve less transport and packaging, and therefore less waste and pollution. And as a bonus, they will taste better.

Landmannalaugar, Iceland

Lifestyle – Have your pet neutered.

Just two cats and their offspring could parent an astonishing 150,000 kittens within 7 years. There are just not enough households willing or able to give homes to this amount of cats. Do your part to prevent the proliferation of domestic animals and have your pet spayed or neutered.

By having your animal neutered, you will be helping to stabilise the populations of stray dogs and cats. When they become too numerous, many unwanted animals are simply abandoned in the street, frequently undergoing great suffering.
www.petrescue.com/spay-neuter.htm

Wayana Indians, Guyana

Energy – Clean the grilles on the back of your refrigerator.

In projected scenarios for 2025, the world production of coal, oil, renewable resources and nuclear power are all expected to remain level or decline. Natural gas is the only energy resource expected to climb in production. Natural gas is closely related to crude oil, and, like crude oil, cannot be replenished on a human timescale. While it gives off far fewer carbon dioxide emissions than crude oil, a number of by-products are of concern such as methane emissions (a potent contributor to the greenhouse effect) and heated water that must be discharged into waterways (thus disrupting fisheries and habitat).

Check your refrigerator's electricity consumption: dust or pet hair on the grilles at the back can cause your compressor to have to work harder, increasing energy use by 30 per cent. Clean them twice a year.

Crevasses, Alaska

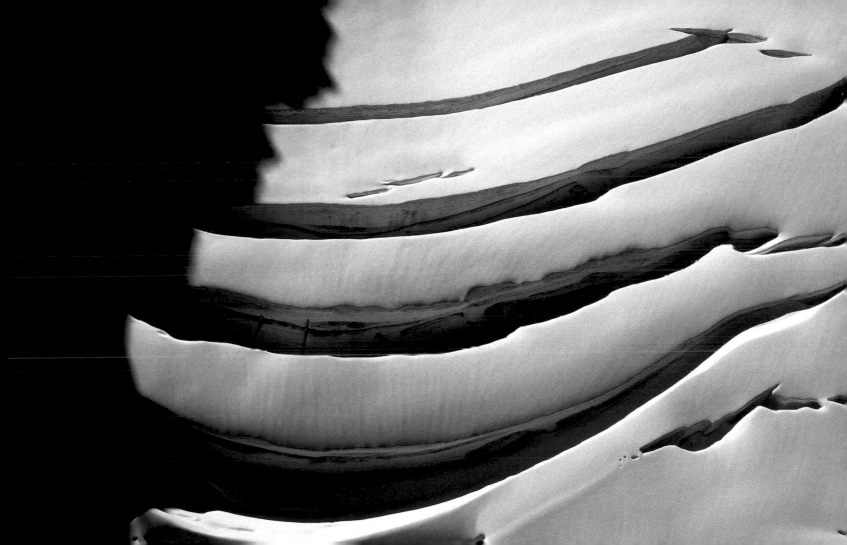

Transport – Use cycle couriers.

With the same materials and resources that it takes to produce a single medium-sized car, 100 bicycles could be produced. On Britain's roads there are nearly 10,000 traffic jams every week, which means 500,000 a year. A quarter of main roads are congested for an hour a day. The cost to business is £20 billion a year.

***

Since riding a bike produces neither greenhouse gases nor pollution, it is one of the best transport solutions. If you run a business and need to deliver mail and parcels regularly around town, use a cycle courier service if one is available. Bikes are quick, being able to bypass traffic jams, and you will be contributing to an improvement in urban air quality in your area.

Pink flamingoes, Kenya

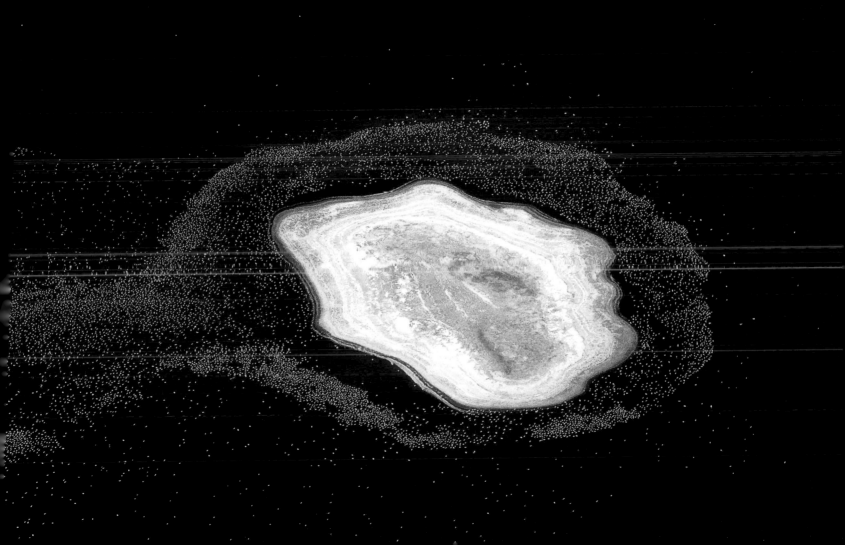

Energy – Reduce the amount of electricity used for lighting.

Electricity for lighting accounts for an average of 15 per cent of your annual electricity bill, and is the second biggest item after refrigeration. By taking a few simple measures, you can save up to 70 per cent of the money you spend on electricity for lighting. You will also help to preserve the earth's energy resources and its atmosphere.

Choose natural light wherever possible, switch off unnecessary lights, and choose bulbs with a wattage that suits your needs. Do not use halogen lights as spotlights but install energy-saving bulbs and fit stairs and passageways with timed- or motion-sensor lights.

Piton de la Fournaise volcano, Réunion

Chemicals – Do not use mothballs in wardrobes.

Mothballs are rather smelly, due to the give naphthalene and para-dichlorobenzene fumes that they give off. The former substance is carcinogenic: repeated, prolonged exposure to high concentrations can damage the nervous system and affect the lungs. Exposure to high levels of naphthalene can cause headaches, fatigue and nausea. Since most of the toxic substances that we use are intended to kill or remove something, so we should not be surprised that they are detrimental to our health.

Use sachets of lavender or cedar chips in your drawers and wardrobes instead of mothballs; they will smell much nicer! Protect delicate woollen items by keeping them in sealed boxes.

Great Barrier Reef, Australia

may 24th

Gardening – Use a hoe to make watering more effective.

Hoeing is one of the most important jobs in the garden as it ensures that water can penetrate the soil surface. After heavy rain, the soil becomes impacted, resulting in a smooth surface that causes water to run off without being able to penetrate. Hoeing helps water to soak into the ground by loosening and breaking up the surface. In addition, well-worked soil drains better and makes watering more efficient by allowing it to filter down to the plant roots that need it.

─────────────

Make sure that when it rains or when you water your garden, none of it will go to waste by putting your hoe to good use.

White Desert, Egypt

Water – Have your house fitted with flow restrictors.

The world's need for water is growing faster than its population. Since 1900, the population has tripled, but world water consumption has risen by twice as much again. Energy production, manufacturing, agriculture and other services in the United Kingdom use 80 per cent of the country's water resources whiled domestic use accounts for 20 per cent.

To reduce your daily consumption, you can fit your taps with flow restrictors for a relatively low cost. If all UK households installed such water-saving features, domestic water use would decrease by 30 per cent.
www.statistics.gov.uk/cci/nugget.asp?id=159

River, Iceland

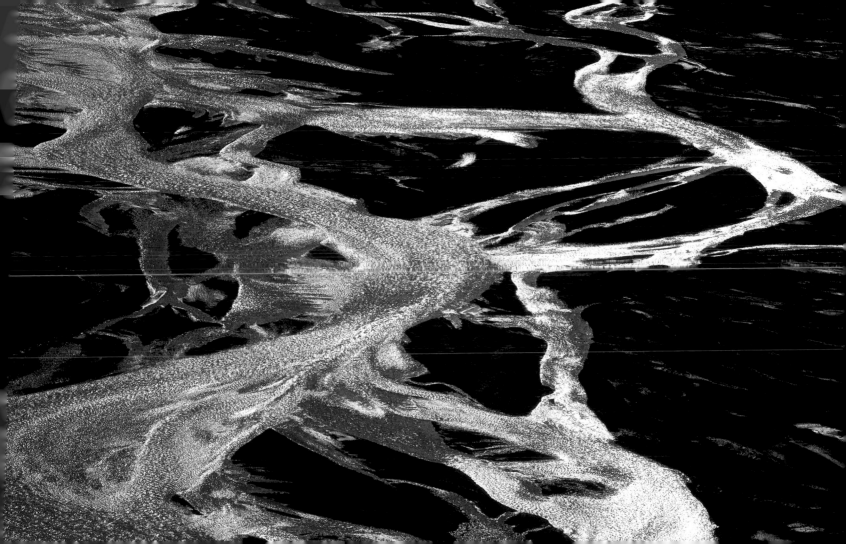

Coral reefs – Have respect for tropical reefs.

Coral reefs play an important part in the life of the ocean. Acting as refuge for prey, a lair for predators, food source, nursery and spawning ground, coral performs many different functions. Despite its appearance, coral is alive, but it grows extremely slowly. It takes coral a year to grow just 10 centimetres. In a fraction of a second, a clumsy kick or blow with a flipper or fin can destroy a coral formation that has been growing for centuries.

If you are on holiday by a tropical lagoon, do not walk on the reef. Take care when diving and never break off a branch of coral to take home as a souvenir.

Coral, Australia

Transport — Make journeys in town by bike.

As astonishing 90 per cent of the world's motor vehicles belong to people living in the world's 16 richest countries, amounting to just a fifth of the global population. However, the effects of car use, especially extreme weather events produced by global warming, are felt all over the world and especially in developing countries, which are generally the most vulnerable. Using a bike to commute to work four days a week for a 12-kilometre round trip would save over 200 litres of fuel annually. If every worker in the United Kingdom did this, our demand for and reliance on oil would plummet.

Cyclists and pedestrians generally breathe in less pollution than car drivers, who breathe in pollution from the car directly in front via the air intake. Go by bike: you will preserve both environmental air quality and your own health.

Ténéré *erg* (sand desert), Niger

Waste – Recycle your steel cans.

Steel is 100 per cent recyclable. One tonne of recycled steel saves the enormous amount of raw materials that are used to produce the same amount of new steel: 1.1 tonnes of iron ore, 54 kilograms of limestone, nearly two-thirds of a tonne of coal and thousands of litres of water.

─────────────

Each of us uses recyclable steel packaging every day in the form of cans. Make sure you put them in your recycling bins; once in the recycling system, they will be transformed into new cans, or sheet metal that is put to various uses – 19,000 steel cans are enough to make a car!

Frozen lake, Greenland

Agriculture – Grow your own vegetables.

Spraying pesticides on crops increases productivity in the short term. Long term, however, the use of chemicals produces resistance in pests, while wiping out their natural predators. The farmer must then increase the dose, exacerbating pollution of the soil, air and water. As a result, the world market in agricultural pesticides has almost tripled in size over the last 20 years.

Rediscover the flavour of something you have grown yourself. A vegetable garden, or just a few vegetables grown in window boxes, will provide you with produce that is free of both pesticides and superfluous packaging. Many vegetables have high levels of pesticide residue when grown conventionally, but can easily be cultivated at home in containers or in your garden.

Volcanic cone, Iceland

Waste – Sort your waste to reduce the amount that needs treating.

In the UK, 8 per cent of rubbish is incinerated. Incineration reduces volume, saves space in landfill sites, and produces energy that can be converted into electricity or heating. However, incineration also produces fumes that contain dioxin (which is carcinogenic), acid gases, and other toxic particles. Anti-pollution regulations demand that incinerators be fitted with filters which, once saturated with toxins, also become waste that requires disposal.

You can reduce air pollution by sorting your waste, such as glass, paper, batteries, engine oil and aluminium cans. These materials can be re-used, and you will be reducing the volume to be incinerated by up to 70 per cent.

Scorpion fish, Australia

Chemicals – Only wash clothes that are really dirty.

The quality of fresh water is constantly deteriorating because of heavy contamination by polluted rain water running off the street, organic matter, and fertilisers and chemical waste from agriculture, industry and individual households. The large amount of waste and toxic products that are poured into rivers daily constitutes a danger that is all the more severe because water consumption, together with the removal of wastewater, is on the increase. In some areas, tap water has to be shut off regularly due to pollution.

It may seem like common sense, but the best way to conserve water when washing the laundry is to do less of it! Only wash your clothes when they are really dirty and need cleaning; one wear does not automatically make clothes dirty.

Geysers, Kamchatka, Russia

Waste – Find out how your local authority manages waste.

Besides the ecological benefits it brings, recycling also creates jobs. Recycling creates 36 jobs per 10,000 tonnes of material recycled, compared to 6 jobs for every 10,000 tonnes sent to traditional disposal facilities.

***

Ask your local authority how it manages your area's waste and what happens to it. Is it put into landfills or burned? Where? If your local authority has not put in place a comprehensive recycling program, ask why. Encourage other people to ask similar questions.

Mud springs, Iceland

Energy – Save energy – do not leave appliances on standby.

In the richest regions of the world, energy consumption per person is on average 10 times that in developing countries, and 4 times the world average. The world average is about 53 billion kilowatt hours (kWh) of electricity per year. Compare this with Ecuador, which uses 9.5 billion kWh. Europeans use 7,000 kWh per person per year.

Power consumption from appliances left on standby (which are therefore not being used) can be as much as 10 per cent of our electricity bill. To switch off your living room appliances – television, video and sound system – plug them into a multi-socket surge protector and switch the surge protector off when you are not using the appliances.

Ounianga Kébir lake, Chad

Leisure – Take the family out cycling.

Between 10 and 30 per cent of children in developed countries are overweight. The reasons for this problem lie in the attraction of television and fast food, and a lack of physical exercise. Make the time to take your children out on a bike ride. Not only will it be beneficial for their health, it is environmentally friendly also and may stimulate their interest in the environment.

Teach your children how to cycle safely and to be aware of the dangers of the close proximity of cars. If you live in a rural area, encourage your children to use their bikes as much as possible, rather than relying on the family car to make short journeys.

Antarctic peninsula

The sea – Look after the seashore.

Contrary to what you might think, the ships that sail the oceans of the world are responsible for only a small part of the sea's pollution. Oil spills account for just 2.5 per cent of pollution and the cleaning of oil tanks at sea by tankers 25 per cent. Most pollution (70 per cent) comes from the land, entering the sea via the waste that is thrown into rivers and streams. In 1996, the authorities on Corsica found a stranded whale with over 3 square metres of plastic sheeting in its stomach.

When you walk along the shore, be sure to leave things as you find them; do not remove rocks or empty shells – they might provide shelter for an animal. The sea and seashore may teem with life but their eco-systems are vulnerable – make sure that children and young people understand the need to respect these habitats.

Whale shark, Australia

Lifestyle – Celebrate the arrival of spring by doing something positive for the world.

Every year, worldwide, nearly 6 million hectares of land become desert. Overgrazing, excessive deforestation, rain and wind erosion and salt contamination are all causes of soil degradation. Already, desertification has affected an area equivalent to the United States and Mexico combined, reducing the land's capacity to support agriculture. The earth will need to be able to feed 8 billion people by 2025, so it is vital that we invest in finding ways to put a stop to desertification and seek to halt the practices that cause it.

The first day of spring falls on either March 20 or 21, on that day, wherever you are in the world day and night are of equal length. Celebrate the coming of spring by deciding to do something positive for the world.

Lava, Kilauea volcano. Hawaii.

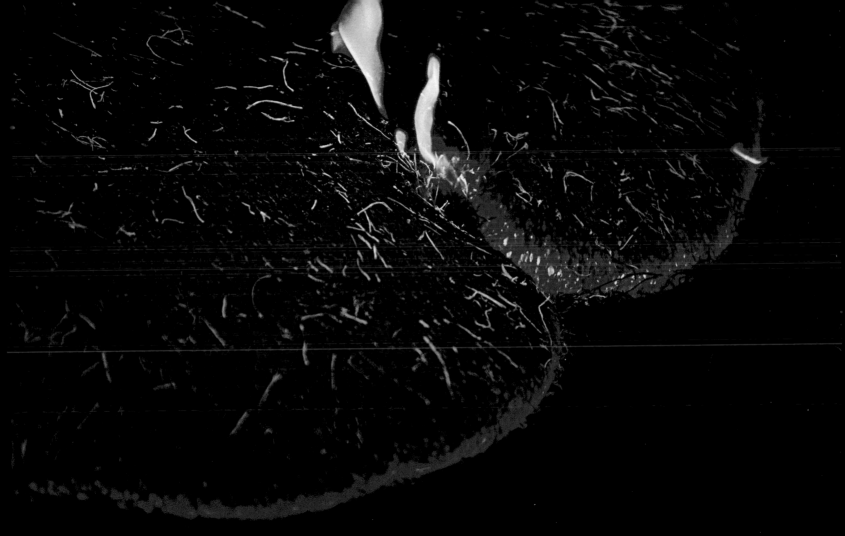

Energy – Save energy when cooking.

In March 2002, an iceberg 53 miles long and 40 miles wide broke off the Antarctic shelf. That same year, the inhabitants of the Tuvalu archipelago in Micronesia began to evacuate their islands as sea levels rose. In order to slow the warming of the seas and the accompanying rise in sea level, we must reduce world emissions of greenhouse gases quickly and drastically. This is all the more urgent because the greenhouse gases already in the atmosphere will continue to have an effect for about 10 years. Global warming will take place no matter what we do.

Be sure always to put a lid on your cooking pots; in this way you can reduce the energy used for cooking by between 20 and 30 per cent. And in addition your food will cook more quickly.

Sandstone, Chad

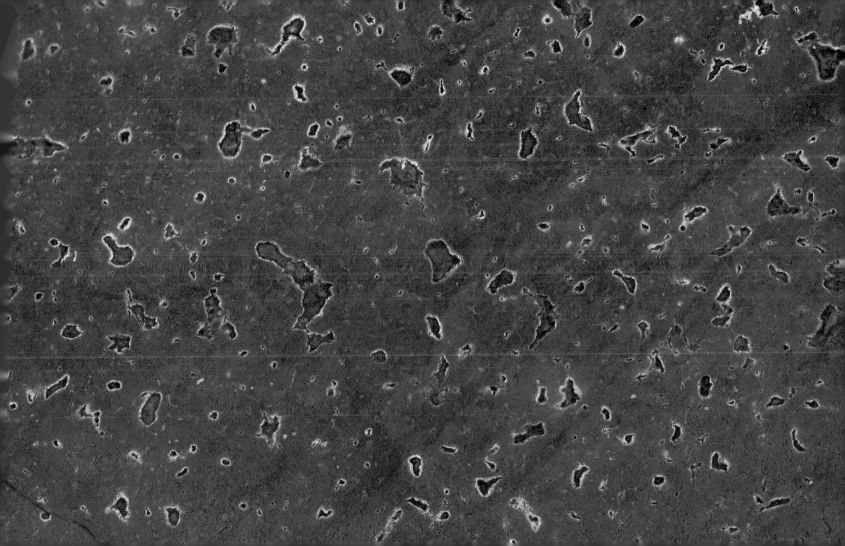

Energy – Unplug your telephone charger.

In 2000, the world used 13 per cent more energy than in 1990. Half of this energy was consumed by 15 per cent of the world's population. In 2020, world energy demand is expected to be one and a half as much again as it is today – that is, 13.5 billion TOE (tonnes of oil equivalent), against 9 billion TOE today. Faced with such forecasts, can we really believe that the damage being done to our natural environment – first and foremost global warming – has any chance of being diminished?

Every little bit counts: by unplugging your mobile phone charger once the battery is fully recharged, you will reduce its energy consumption.

Mount Pinatubo, Philippines

Biodiversity – Make sure you have the necessary paperwork to import a protected species.

At present the Convention on International Trade in Endangered Species of Wild Flora and Fauna (CITES) prohibits the trade of more 800 animal and plant species, including tigers, turtles and rhinoceroses, and controls that of a further 25,000 species – such as coral, cactuses, parrots, reptiles and orchids, as well as animal skins and shells – via a system of permits.

When travelling, make sure you do not buy souvenirs made from animal or plant species whose trade has been forbidden internationally, and obtain a permit if one is required. Contact the UK branch of CITES for more information.
www.ukcites.gov.uk

Pelican, Galápagos Islands

Leisure – Take a holiday where equitable tourism is promoted.

Tourism is now the world's biggest industry and there is a wealth of exotic destinations in glossy brochures from which to choose. However, developing countries often gain little financial benefit from the influx of visitors to their shores: only around 30 per cent of the money spent by tourists on their holiday remains in the host country, but equitable tourism is promoted in some countries.

It is worth paying a little more, if you can afford to do so and if you are sure the money will be put to good use – contributing towards a fairer wages for local workers, finance for healthy drinking water supplies and support for humanitarian activities. Organised trips show visitors what local conditions are really like. You will be able to see that your money can be put to good use.

Great Barrier Reef, Australia

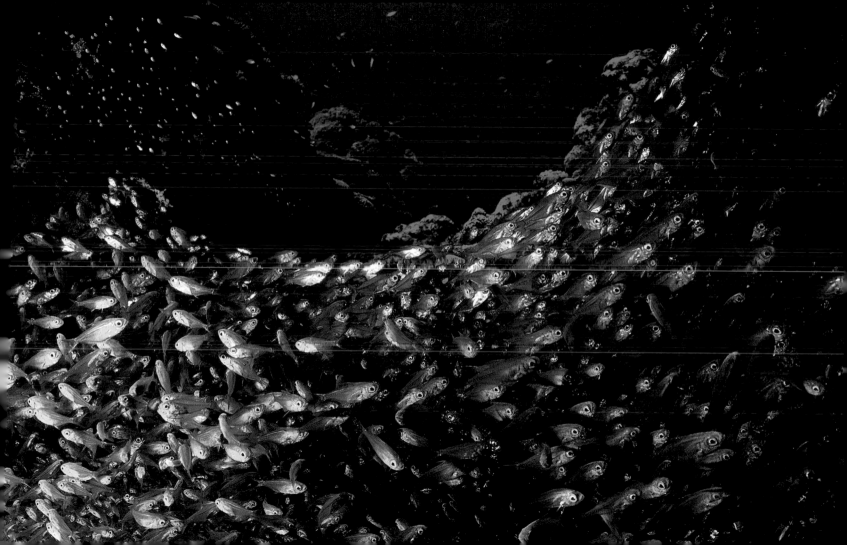

Transport – Do not drive your car on very hot days.

The city of Los Angeles suffers severe pollution on 150 days of each year. Poor air quality in cities is caused by polluting gases such as tropospheric ozone, the main ingredient of photo-chemical smog, which can cause breathing difficulties. It is formed at ground level from the reaction of car exhaust gases as they emerge into sunlight and heat.

On very hot days, drive more slowly. Better still, leave the car in the garage on most days. Invest the money you save in maintaining your bicycle or buying a nice pair of running shoes. With the money you will save, you can afford both!

Ounianga Kébir lake, Chad

june 11th

Energy – Install your boiler close to where hot water is used.

Thanks to the sun, the wind, rivers and geothermal energy, we are able to tap the earth's renewable energy sources, which neither pollute nor produce waste that can threaten the future of the earth or the generations to come. If we were to use the best available technology in buildings, on transport, industry, food and services, global energy use could be halved. Until this technology is widely used, however, we should not forget that the smartest way to use energy is to use as little of it as possible.

Position your boiler close to the hot water's exit points – such as the kitchen and bathroom – to reduce heat loss (and therefore waste of energy) through pipes.

Hot springs, Iceland

Forests – Give preference to locally produced wood.

Around one million hectares of forest in the United Kingdom is certified by the Forest Stewardship Council, while worldwide, 24,470,898 hectares fall under this scheme. FSC-certification guarantees that the wood was grown and harvested in an environmentally responsible, socially beneficial and economically viable manner.

Do not use exotic woods for furniture and carpentry. Instead, rediscover chestnut, oak, pine, fir, and beech: they can be treated to make them extremely tough. As well as protecting the tropical rainforest, the need for polluting transportation will be avoided.

Kokerbooms (or 'quiver trees'), Namibia

Energy – Clean your air conditioner filter.

Since 1850, the industrial revolution in the West has led to a sharp increase in our energy requirements, which have grown relentlessly due to the combined effects of rising standards of living and population growth. The growth of any sphere of activity is accompanied by a growth in energy consumption; it is rising at 2.7 per cent per year in developing countries and is expected to continue to do so until 2025, while in the industrialised world, the rate is 1.2 per cent per year and in Eastern Europe and the former Soviet Union demand is expected to average 1.5 per cent per year until 2025.

If you really must use air conditioning, never do so with open doors or windows.
Regularly check that it is working properly and that the filter is clean, to avoid any excess energy consumption.

Ice floe, Greenland

The sea – If you fish from the shore, be sure to take all your fishing line home with you.

More than 3 billion people, 60 per cent of the world's population, live less than 50 miles from the coast, and 6 of the world's 8 largest cities are situated close to the sea. In 30 years time, 6 billion people, or 75 per cent of the world's population, will live by the sea. Effluent from agriculture, industry and domestic households, is already building up along coastlines and levels will inevitably increase. As they do so, fish stocks will be poisoned and seashore habitats destroyed, killing the species that live there.

If you fish from the shore, always make sure you take all your nylon fishing line home with you, even if it is broken. It poses a great threat to wildlife and can also get caught in the propellers of boats.

Andaman Sea, India

june 15th

Waste – Choose products sold in glass containers, rather than plastic.

Glass is an excellent material for recycling: it can be re-used or recycled indefinitely, with no loss of either weight or quality. Unlike paper, the primary benefit of recycling glass comes not from protecting the original source of the material, but rather conserving the energy it would take to create the new material. Recycled glass melts at a much lower temperature than the raw materials used to make new glass, thus using less energy.

Cooking oil is available in both non-recyclable plastic bottles and in glass bottles that can be recycled endlessly. You know which one you should choose!

Ténéré Desert, Niger

Water – Drink tap water.

The world market for bottled water, estimated at US$35 billion per year, is flourishing. In the United Kingdom, 53 per cent of adults drink bottled water, worth £1,200 million in sales. However, the most natural of all drinks is much less natural once it is packaged. To contain the world's bottled water, 1.5 million tonnes of plastic are required. Manufacturing the bottles, packing and transporting the water (a quarter of this water is drunk outside its country of origin) uses natural resources and energy, and generates mountains of waste because most plastic bottles are not recycled.

Do not forget that our tap water is treated so as to be perfectly drinkable and its quality is checked rigorously. In addition, it is between 240 and 10,000 times cheaper than bottled water.

Reflection, Australia

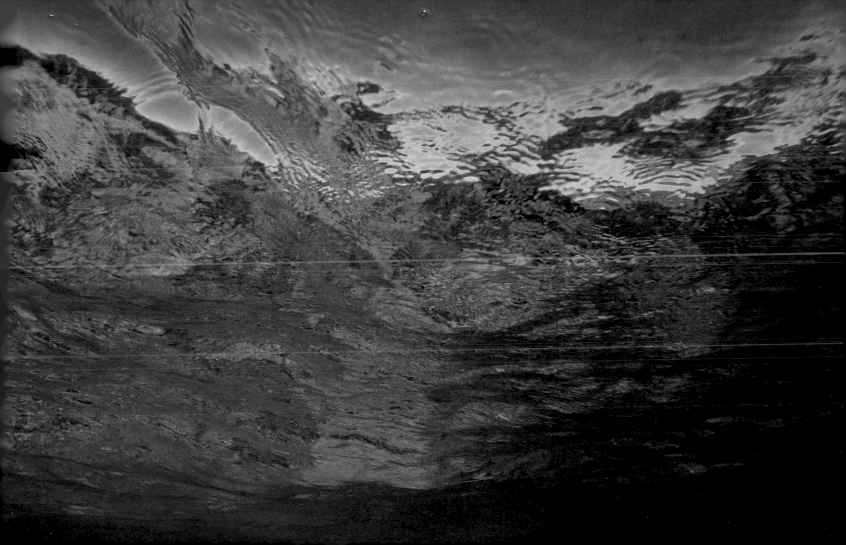

The sea – Take care not to harm any forms of life when diving.

The slight rise in sea temperature that has occurred in recent years (caused by global warming) can be enough to interfer with the growth of coral, causing it to lose the algae which gives it its colour and become bleached. The coral can sometimes recover, but if the stress to which it has been subjected is too severe or if it has gone on for too long, between 10 per cent and 30 per cent can die. When the coral dies, the fish and plants living on the reef also suffer.

If you dive on or near a coral reef be very careful. It is very easy to damage the coral when swimming with flippers; the kicking action of your legs can dislodge pieces of it. Do not touch the coral and swim with care. Do not attempt to feed any fish or other sea creatures, or interfere with them in any way.

Nudibranches (sea slugs), Australia

Transport – Take part in National Bike Week.

UK cycling activists first started Bike Week in 1923. Normally taking place in June, it holds over 2,000 local biking events with over 300,000 participants all over the UK and is a celebration of cycling. Launched in 1996, the National Cycling Strategy aims to encourage a culture that favours the increased use of the bike for all age groups and to quadruple the number of cycle trips that were made in the year of its launch by the year 2012. This would bring the level of cycle use in the United Kingdom up to the levels of Germany and Sweden.

The committed cyclist does not need to wait for Bike Week in order to take to the roads, but if you are a fair-weather cyclist, use it as an excuse to service your bike before summer arrives. If you cannot service it yourself, take it to a cycle shop. They might also offer free or cheap maintenance classes, or evening classes might be available locally.
www.ctc.org.uk/
www.bikeweek.org.uk/

Gulf of Goubbet, Djibouti

The sea – When on holiday, support the Blue Flag scheme.

Every year, billions of gallons of wastewater from towns and cities is allowed to flow into the sea, but three-quarters of this water has not been treated. In Europe, to keep marine pollution in check, the Blue Flag scheme is in operation. It is awarded annually to those holiday resorts and local authorities who succeed in maintaining good water quality, and who educate and inform the public about environmental management and safety. The Blue Flag's high profile acts as an incentive to local authorities, since it is in their interests commercially to earn and keep this award.

Look for the Blue Flag when choosing your holiday destination. In 2004, it was awarded to almost 3,000 beaches and marinas in 29 countries.

Andaman Island, India

Biodiversity – Protect each habitat, from wetland to forest.

At present, a quarter of the earth's mammal species, an eighth of birds, a third of fish and probably more than half of all flowering plants and insects are threatened with extinction. It is not enough to protect the species themselves, their habitats need to be preserved as well. Worldwide, 12 per cent of the land surface is now protected in this way, having doubled over the past 10 years. Likewise, bodies of water are supplied by watersheds – the area of land that drains into the body of water – and in order to protect the quality of water and habitat, we must consider what happens on the land that drains to it. Approaching environmental problems and solutions holistically is the best method for solving such problems in the long term.

Discover the breathtaking landscapes and wild species of Britain's national parks and waterways. But don't forget that protecting nature demands both curiosity and restraint. Respect the rules of these protected areas.

Mount St Helens National Volcanic Monument, United States

Energy – Do not make excessive use of the tumble dryer.

At present 15 per cent of the world's energy comes from renewable sources. This share could rise to 40 per cent if wind, solar, hydro-electric and biomass energy were developed, reducing the pollution produced by burning fossil fuels and from creating nuclear power. Worldwide, the number of photovoltaic installations (solar panels) increased by 927 megawatts in 2004, from 574 megawatts the year before.

Of all household electrical appliances, the tumble dryer consumes the most energy. It uses twice, or even three times as much power as a washing machine. The cheapest and most environmentally friendly way of drying the washing will always be to hang it out to dry in the air.

Tassili n'Adjer, Algeria

Energy – Choose a supplier that subscribes to a renewable resources scheme.

Each time you use an electrical appliance or light, natural resources are used to generate the electricity that powers it. A massive 98 per cent of the electricity produced in America comes from traditional, non-renewable resources, which are the number one cause of industrial air pollution in the US. The remaining 2 per cent is generated from renewable resources such as geothermal, small hydro and biomass resources, solar energy and wind.

The TREC (Tradable Renewable Energy Certificate) is a scheme that aims to promote renewable power generation, but has yet to be adopted worldwide. Contact your energy supplier to find out if they subscribe to a renewable resources scheme.

Altiplano, Bolivia

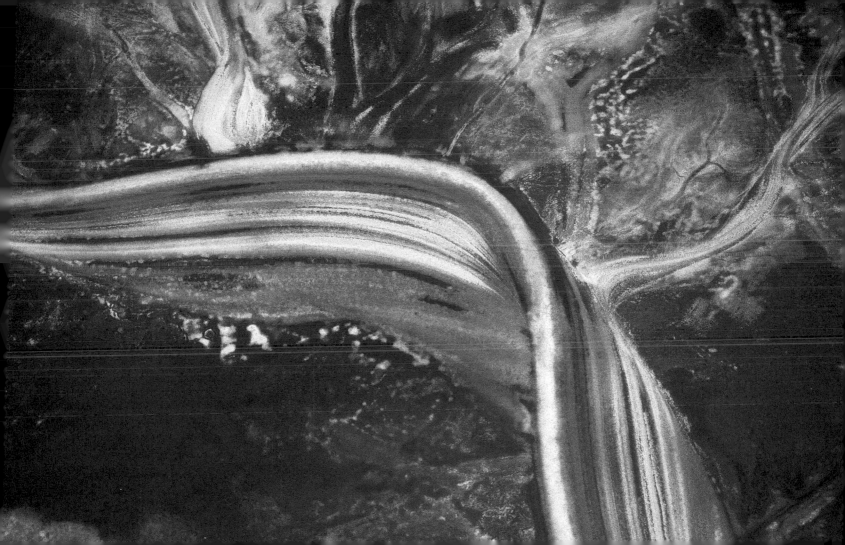

The sea – Ask for the MSC (Marine Stewardship Council) label.

Fish stocks are in free-fall across the seas of the world, having dropped by a third in less than 30 years. Certification labels encourage good practice by identifying products that come from sustainably managed fisheries; that is, from areas where efforts are made to preserve the natural marine environment and the richness of species, while guaranteeing a decent wage for fishermen. Consumers can therefore encourage ecologically responsible fishing practices by buying approved products.

Look for seafood products bearing the Marine Stewardship Council label. The MSC is an independent, non-profit making global organisation that promotes seafood that is produced sustainably.

Piton de la Fournaise volcano, Réunion

Energy – Do not use air conditioning to excess.

The world's energy consumption is increasing relentlessly as standards of living rise. Air conditioning, is particularly energy voracious. If used to excess (that is, to produce a cold rather than a comfortable temperature), it wastes large quantities of electricity.

—————————

Set air conditioning to a temperature 5 degrees below the temperature outside. By being content with a degree or two less, you can save up to 10 per cent of daily energy consumption. Use it in moderation in your car as well.

Glacial corridor, Greenland

june 25th

Transport – Choose a trailer rather than a roof rack to transport goods.

A roof rack on a car contributes to pollution and climate change. When loaded, it increases wind resistance by up to 15 per cent, which is reflected in increased fuel consumption as the engine needs more power to counteract the wind resistance. Even when empty, a roof rack increases fuel consumption by 10 per cent when travelling at the same speed.

─────────────

If you have to carry a lot of luggage when you go on holiday or need to transport bulky goods, use a trailer, or send bags, bikes and surfboards on ahead by train, which will produce less pollution. If you must use a roof rack, remove it when not in use.

Blizzard on the ice cap, Greenland

Energy – Decide what you want before you open the fridge door.

Replacing a 10-year old refrigerator bought in 1990 with a new European Energy A-rated model would save enough energy to light the average household for over 3 months. In a well-equipped household, the fridge alone accounts for a third of electricity consumption (20 per cent for the freezer and 12 per cent for the refrigerator).

In order not to increase your already high energy consumption needlessly, close the refrigerator door as soon as you have taken out what you need. Every time you open it, up to 30 per cent of the cooled air can escape. And remember that the tidier the inside, the less time the door needs to be kept open.

Iceberg, Greenland

Lifestyle – Spread the word and make the people around you aware of environmental problems.

Not everyone has the same level of awareness of environmental problems. It is generally agreed, however, that the world's natural resources need to be looked after and preserved. It is up to all of us to make sure that the urgency of the problem is understood.

―――――――――――――

Spread the word and help family, friends, neighbours and colleagues to become aware of the need to conserve natural resources and keep the environment healthy. Encourage them to take action, no matter how small, to look after the earth.

Animal footprints in ash, Philippines

Agriculture – Reduce your meat consumption and help reduce the global appetite.

It takes 1,500 litres of water to produce one kilogram of cereal, but 15,000 litres to produce one kilogram of beef. Two-thirds of the grain produced each year, enough to feed 2 billion people, are destined for livestock feed in the United States and Europe. Worldwide, over half the grain grown is fed to animals, rather than people. This system, which is too costly in natural resources including water, soil and energy sources, will not be able to sustain the 8 billion people estimated to be living on earth in 2030.

If your diet is rich in meat, reduce your consumption. You will be helping to relieve a small part of the pressures of our global appetite.
www.news.cornell.edu/Chronicle/97/8.14.97/livestock.html

Cayman, Venezuela

june 29th

Water – Do not waste water where it is scarce.

In a developing country such as Thailand, a golf course uses 1,497 kilograms of chemical fertiliser, herbicides and pesticides, which pollute the soil and water resources. It also uses as much water as 60,000 villagers or 6,000 residents of Bangkok.

———————

When you travel in tropical lands, in order to save water your hotel may offer to not wash your sheets and towels every day, but only when you ask. Support such schemes.

Namib Desert, Namibia

Energy – Do not leave electrical chargers plugged in once their appliance has been removed.

We all love cordless appliances, they make life so much easier; from the cordless phone, electric kettle and hand-held vacuum to the mobile phone, pager and PDA (personal digital assistant). But all these devices need to be charged before they can be used. The types of charger vary, some reduce their consumption of electricity to a trickle once the appliance has been removed, but others continue to draw 2 to 6 watts of power even after the appliance is fully charged.

Remember to switch off the power to your electrical chargers while they are not in use, and look for the specification '-dV', which indicates that the charger will reduce its energy use when it is not charging an appliance.

Icebergs, Greenland

july 1st

Gardening – Boil water to kill weeds.

It is now known that, because they contain harmful chemicals, using too much of products such as fertiliser, insecticide, herbicide and fungicide on crops damages the environment, and especially the water supply. However, most of us are guilty of using these products in our own gardens, which produces exactly the same kind of pollution.

You can dispense with chemical herbicide, for example, by using boiling water. Weeds that have had boiling water poured over them will turn brown within a few hours and subsequently die. The effect is similar to a contact herbicide but there is no toxic residue and the area is immediately safe for children to play.

Acacia, Niger

Transport – Take the train rather than the car.

Most people start their working day or holiday in a car, fighting traffic, frustration and boredom. A passenger on a train, whether travelling for business or pleasure, can move about freely throughout the train, sleep, read or chat with their fellow passengers. Most people in the UK use a car to get around. In 2002, 73 per cent of trips were made by car, 12 per cent by train and 4 per cent by coach.

Discover the comfort of train travel. Your journey will be less tiring and safer, and you will reduce your contribution to global warming considerably.

Stalactites, Greenland

Chemicals – Use phosphate-free washing detergents.

Phosphates, contained in some detergents such as washing powders and tablets, are used to counteract the effect of hard water. Their introduction into the environment produces an excessively high concentration of nutrients, a sort of 'over-fertilisation' that causes excessive growth of algae and the progressive asphyxiation of animal and plant life (eutrophication). As a result, algae are choking our rivers and water supplies.

Washing powder manufacturers now add smaller quantities of phosphate to their products, but this action is not enough to save our water. Be eco-friendly and buy products that are phosphate-free.

Hot springs, Kamchatka, Russia

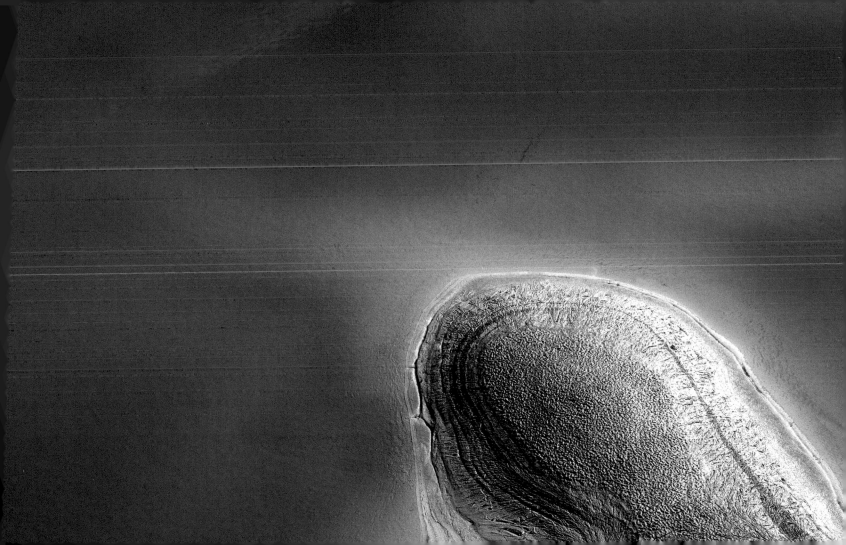

july 4th

Waste – Recycle ink cartridges.

Every year 40 million laser printer and inkjet cartridges are sold in the United Kingdom; of these, 30 to 40 per cent are recycled or remanufactured. Made of plastic, iron, and aluminium, none of which is biodegradable, printer cartridges can be re-used up to 50 times. Recycling cartridges is common sense; yet 12,000 to 14,000 tonnes end up in landfill sites every year.

Contribute to the growth of recycling by handing in your used cartridges and urging your employer to do the same. There are also organisations that collect them and use the proceeds for humanitarian or educational purposes.

Blue octopus, Australia

Waste – Dispose of bulky items correctly.

How should you dispose of awkward items such as domestic appliances, furniture, garden waste, sheets of metal, tyres and anything else that will not fit into the dustbin? We all need to dispose of bulky items from time to time. Contact your local authority to find out about recycling or collection services. A charity might be able to recycle the item for you, although certain furniture items will need to have a fire retardant certificate.

———————

Items that have been dumped illegally on wasteland or in the street create an eyesore and pose a problem for the local authority that has to remove them. Dispose of large items legally at local authority amenity sites, or call them for advice.

Namib Desert, Namibia

Waste – Say 'no' to disposable products.

Disposable products have invaded our day-to-day life. Paper napkins, paper plates, paper tablecloths, plastic razors, plastic cigarette lighters and plastic cups: items are used once, then thrown away! As well as increasing the volume of rubbish, disposable products waste the energy used to make and transport them. It is not difficult to do without disposables, since each has a reusable – and therefore sustainable and more environmentally friendly – alternative. Often, this is considerably cheaper, too.

A household in which a broom and a sponge are used for cleaning spends around £20 per year on these items. Using disposable wipes would cost more than £300.

Tungurahua volcano, Ecuador

Leisure – Look for the Green Globe 21 certification when making your holiday choices.

Based on Agenda 21 and the principles for sustainable development endorsed by 182 heads of state at the United Nations Rio de Janeiro Earth Summit, Green Globe 21 provides companies, participating countries and consumers with an independent, certifying standard for sustainable tourism. It certifies everything from accommodation and adventure activities to golf courses and vineyards, ensuring that ecologically sustainable development principles and practices are observed and applied. Participating organisations are re-evaluated every year.

Use companies and organisations displaying the Green Globe 21 logo, which attempt to leave fewer harmful traces on our world.

Glacier National Park, United States

Water – If you don't like tap water, use a filter.

Tap water in the United Kingdom is of high quality and is very safe to drink. Whether from reservoirs, rivers, or boreholes, all water has to pass through one of the UK's 2,500 water treatment plants. At these plants, the water goes through a clarification, filtration and disinfection process – a chemical is added to the 'raw' water and the pollutants float to the top or sink to the bottom. Filtration removes the smaller particles, and finally the addition of chlorine disinfects the water and kills all bacteria.

To reduce the chlorine taste in water, you can install a filter on the tap, or add a few drops of lemon juice in your jug. Or, simpler still, place the water jug in the refrigerator for a few hours: chlorine is volatile and will evaporate.

White Desert, Egypt

Noise – Reduce the amount of noise you make in your neighbourhood.

Noise is part of our environment and plays a significant role in our quality of life. In the UK, researchers at Sheffield University found that British cities are up to 10 times noisier today than they were 10 years ago. Yet, 75 per cent of formal noise complaints made in England and Wales in 2002/2003 related to domestic noise, that is to say, noisy neighbours.

Noise pollution has clear effects on our bodies, causing lack of sleep, irritability, indigestion and high blood pressure. Be aware of the sound level in your home or work environments and make an effort to eliminate as much noise as possible.
www.swenvo.org.uk/environment/Sec_nuisance.asp

Sandstone, Chad

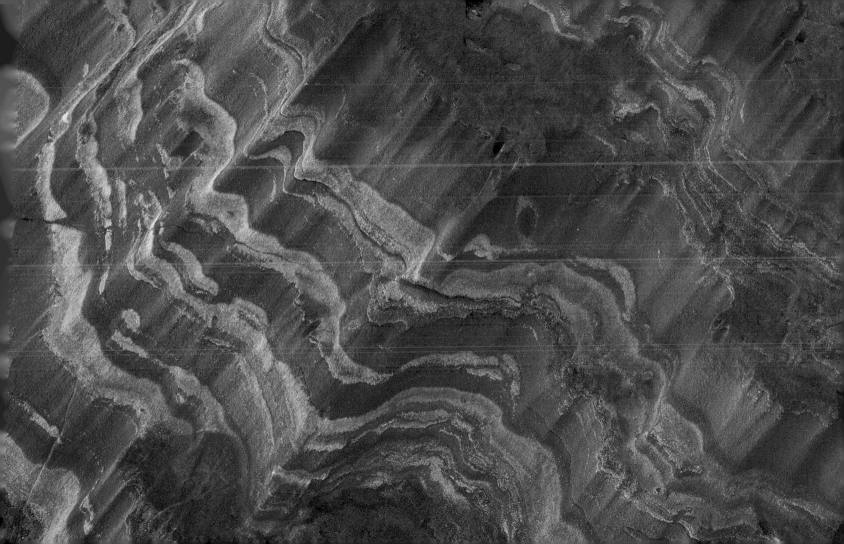

Biodiversity – Do not buy souvenirs made from protected species.

Over-exploitation of living creatures – due to hunting, fishing, or excessive harvesting – is one of the main causes of species extinction. When a species is protected and yet trade in it continues, it is known as trafficking. Illegal trade in threatened animal and plant species is the third biggest form of trafficking in the world after arms and drugs; this trade affects 13 per cent of the bird and mammal species that are threatened with extinction.

_____

By buying products or souvenirs that are made from protected species, you are encouraging this trade and are speeding up the extinction of species. Before you buy goods to take home from trips abroad, check with the authorities of the countries concerned (such as the consulate, customs, or environment ministry) to make sure that you do not choose anything made from a protected species.

Elephants, Kenya

Waste – Return used batteries.

Power is produced inside a battery by a chemical reaction being converted into electrical energy. Most conventional cylindrical and button batteries, such as those used to power radios, torches, cameras, etc., contain toxic metals such as cadmium, mercury, lead and nickel, all of which are extremely harmful to the environment. Even though some newer batteries can be disposed of in household rubbish, it is strongly recommended that you recycle alkaline batteries.

Many large commercial shops accept batteries for recycling. They may not advertise the fact, so ask the manager if you are unsure. You can also ask the manufacturer for advice on recycling. Ideally, limit the number or products that you use that require batteries and buy a battery charger and rechargeable batteries. More expensive initially, it will be cheaper in the long run.

Erosion, Kamchatka, Russia

Chemicals – Make less use of air conditioning in your car.

CFCs (chlorofluorocarbons), the gases used in aerosols, refrigerators and air conditioners, are destroying the ozone layer, arousing fears of a resurgence in the incidence of skin cancer. However, it now appears that the hole in the ozone layer above the southern hemisphere, which reached epic proportions at the end of 2000 being 3 times the size of the United States, has now stabilised. Even though most countries quickly banned CFCs and replaced them with alternatives, leading to a 10 per cent reduction in their manufacture within 10 years, the CFCs already in the atmosphere will continue to have a damaging effect for several decades to come.

Between 15 and 20 percent of coolant gas escapes from car air conditioners, adding to the damage being inflicted upon the ozone layer. Do you really need to use air conditioning in your car? Surely opening the windows and sunroof is just as refreshing?

Ice floe, Alaska

Forests – Do not light fires in the forest.

Carbon dioxide emissions are one of the chief sources of the air pollution that is causing the proven disturbance in our climate. They are produced chiefly by the burning of the fossil fuels – coal, oil and gas – which we use to meet our energy requirements. Forest fires are another major source of the carbon dioxide emissions that are released into the atmosphere, when the carbon dioxide absorbed by the trees during photosynthesis is released. Some fires are caused accidentally, but equally many are started deliberately to clear vast areas for agriculture.

In 2002, 2.5 million hectares of the world's forest and wildlife habitat was destroyed by forest fires. Preserve the earth's forests. Do not light fires.

Patagonia, Argentina

Biodiversity – Beware of invasive species. Do not introduce non-native plants or animals into your environment.

The balance of the species living in each habitat is very delicate. Any foreign species that are introduced, either accidentally or deliberately, could find conditions so favourable that they become invasive. Miconia, an ornamental bush introduced into Tahiti in 1937, now covers two thirds of the island. Caulerpa, a tropical seaweed, monotonously blankets vast areas of the Mediterranean. The water hyacinth, originally from Brazil, chokes rivers in Africa. The grey squirrel, introduced into the UK around 1900, spread rapidly, displacing the native red squirrel from most of England and Wales. In Hawaii, the Indian mongoose was released to eradicate rats in the sugar cane fields. The mongoose did nothing to slow the proliferation of rats, but instead destroyed most of the local native flora and fauna, driving many species close to extinction.

To avoid an ecological disaster, do not release any non-native species into the environment and never smuggle plants or animals home in your luggage.

Niger River, Mali

The sea – Do not eat swordfish.

North Atlantic swordfish, the type found in most restaurants and supermarkets, have been severely overfished. At the start of the 20th century, the average swordfish weighed around 160 kilograms while today, just 100 years later, the average fish weighs just 40 kilograms. Swordfish stocks are currently at the lowest level ever recorded. Over half of the swordfish caught and sold are young fish that haven't had the chance to reproduce.

Do not buy swordfish to eat at home or choose it in a restaurant. It is simply too much at risk from today's intensive fishing methods.

Banc d'Arguin, Mauritania

Waste – Take your rubbish with you.

Some waste is biodegradable, which means that it decomposes easily in the environment. Other waste decomposes over longer periods. A tissue takes 3 months to decompose, a piece of paper takes 4 months, chewing gum takes 5 years, a can decomposes over 10 years, a plastic bottle takes at least 100 years and a glass bottle several centuries.

———

No matter how long something takes to decompose, do not leave your waste behind: always take it with you and put it in a dustbin, or better yet, a recycling bin.

Old volcanic cone, Bolivia

Chemicals – Choose solvents made from plants.

Solvents are powerful enough to dissolve other substances: they attack fats, and keep certain products liquid, such as glues and paints. Most solvents are organic (acetone, ether, white spirit) and belong to the family of volatile organic compounds (VOCs). White spirit is one of the most deadly solvents. It is harmful if touched or inhaled.

For decorating, maintenance or DIY jobs, use plant-based solvents, which are less harmful to the environment – for example, turpentine and other products made from terpenes, which you can buy in health stores.

Mantis shrimp, Australia

Construction – Choose solar-powered heating for your home.

Renewable energy sources such as solar power do not produce greenhouse gases and their reserves are inexhaustible – so why not heat your house and water with power of the sun? Many people are under the impression that solar heating is only effective in tropical regions, but this is not the case. It can be effective in a European climate too. Depending on the circumstances, solar energy can supply 40 to 80 per cent of hot water needs and 20 to 40 per cent of heating requirements. A solar hot water heater can therefore make savings of 40 to 70 per cent in energy consumption during the summer.

Grants for renewable energy sources are available from the government for solar-powered systems (for both business and domestic use) that are connected to the national grid. But if you do not qualify for a grant, it is still worth considering installing solar panels; they will normally pay for themselves in around 12 years.

Ice crystals, Greenland

Lifestyle – Give your time to an environmental organisation.

The UK boasts a large array of environmental organisations – local, regional and national. Some focus on the issue of access to resources, some on environmental responsibility, others on public education, and many on all three. In order to lend financial support to the initiatives of these organisations, some people choose to donate money or subscribe as members, whereas others give up their spare time to take part in environmental activities and initiatives.

These organisations have a great deal to contribute. They also need your help. Investigate the environmental groups in your area, and support their work in some way.

Piton de la Fournaise volcano, Réunion

Leisure – Be environmentally friendly on camping trips.

You might think that there is relatively little you can do to harm the environment when camping, but this kind of activity leaves its mark on nature too. The soil beneath the tent becomes compressed and vegetation in the surrounding area disturbed. Always pitch your tent in designated camping grounds.

———

The timing of your holiday is also important. If you choose a popular destination for your trip, choose to go at less busy times of year, having fewer people around will not only add to the enjoyment of your trip but also reduces the impact on the environment on any given day.

Olympic National Park, United States

Leisure – Make your children aware of the natural world that surrounds them.

Make your children aware of nature and the environment to stimulate their interest in protecting it. Inaction is often due to ignorance rather than negligence. The children of today will soon have the earth's future in their hands. Let us work towards giving them the means to do better tomorrow than we have done today.

———————

Get your children interested in nature. Take them into the countryside, visit an environmental centre or a botanical garden. Buy a field guide, magnifying glass and binoculars and encourage them to study insects and flowers or to watch birds, and to draw and record their findings. Get them accustomed to taking part in open-air activities. By broadening their interests, you will help to increase their awareness and can learn a lot yourself.

Sea crocodile, Australia

Transport – Keep your tyres properly inflated.

Keeping tyres fully inflated reduces wear and tear on them and increases longevity, thereby saving money. It also saves precious raw material: it takes 27 litres of crude oil to produce a new tyre. Under-inflated tires can increase fuel consumption by up to 10 per cent. Around the world, millions of litres of petrol a day are used needlessly by driving with low-pressure tyres.

Take care to keep your car tyres at the pressure recommended by the manufacturer. Check your tyres once a month, it will be 5 minutes well spent.

Glacier, Greenland

Chemicals – Buy a refrigerator that does not damage the ozone layer or the climate.

International measures for halting the destruction of the ozone layer stipulate that chlorofluorocarbons (CFCs) in refrigeration equipment must be replaced by hydrochlorofluorocarbons (HCFCs) and hydrofluorocarbons (HFCs), which do not damage the ozone layer. Unfortunately, however, HCFCs and HFCs still contribute significantly to climate change due to the chlorine they contain, which makes them far more powerful greenhouse gases than carbon dioxide itself. The increase in the use of HFCs expected by 2050 will contribute as much to global warming as the emissions from all the cars in the world added together.

––––––––––

Refrigerators are available that do not contain CFCs or HCFCs – they use isobutene instead. When you replace your refrigerator, do some research into models that neither damage the ozone layer nor contribute to climate change.

Uzon caldera, Kamchatka, Russia

Chemicals – Use the correct amount of detergents and other cleaning agents.

Thanks to the efforts made by washing detergent manufacturers, far less detergent is now required to wash a load of laundry or dishes.

Check the packages for the recommended doses for whatever you are washing (especially if you are using concentrated detergents), and ensure that you follow them. Using more does not give better results and is more costly, and wastes more packaging and therefore natural resources. Excess detergent also contributes to the degradation of rivers that are already polluted.

Iceberg, Greenland

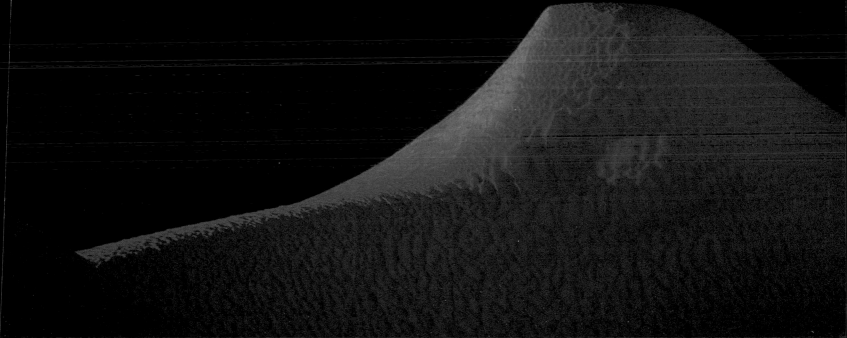

Agriculture – Choose organic cotton.

The cultivation of cotton accounts for only 2.5 per cent of the world's farmed land, but it uses 25 per cent of the world's pesticides, making cotton the most pollution-causing crop. Industrial processing of the raw fibres is equally harmful to the environment; it involves bleaching with chlorine and the use of dyes made with heavy metals that are harmful to people and the environment. Grown without the use of pesticides, organic cotton restores fertility to the soil and preserves the balance of ecosystems. It is harvested by hand and processed without the use of chemical treatments.

——————————

Choosing organic cotton will contribute to your well-being, and to the well-being of those who grow the crop, while safeguarding the environment.
www.pan-uk.org/Cotton/cotindex.htm

Sangay volcano, Ecuador

july 26th

The sea – Do not throw waste into the ocean.

An astonishing 265 million tonnes of all kinds of waste lies at the bottom of the Mediterranean. A newspaper takes 6 weeks to decompose in the sea and a cardboard box takes 3 months, but some of the waste will remain for centuries. A cigarette end takes 2 years to decompose, but a steel can takes 80 years. An aluminium can will last 100 years and a plastic bag 300. A piece of polystyrene or a plastic bottle will still be around in 500 years time. Glass lasts even longer.

————————————

Vast though it is, the sea cannot be a dumping ground for all our waste. Do not leave waste on the shore or throw any overboard while at sea.

Elephant crossing a sea channel, Andaman Islands, India

The sea – Do not eat rare fish species at home or choose them in a resturant.

Consumption of fish has more than doubled in the last fifty years. Today, 47 per cent of the world's commercial marine stocks are being fished to the limit of their capacity, 15 per cent are being over-fished and 10 per cent of stocks have already been exhausted or are building up again slowly – in the waters off Newfoundland, cod stocks are struggling to recover despite a moratorium on fishing. A modern factory ship can catch as much cod in an hour as a typical fishing boat could land in an entire season in the 16th century. Only a quarter of the world's fish stocks are moderately fished or under-fished, and species that were once plentiful have become rare.

Be careful about what fish you choose. Many species are now threatened by being fished into extinction, including bluefin tuna, cod, hake, monkfish, sole, Atlantic salmon, pollack and herring, and many more.

Shoal of bonitos, Australia

Consumption – Make out a shopping list and buy what you need rather than what you want

We are easily tempted by something we 'want'. We rarely stop to ask ourselves what we 'need'. If everyone on earth were to live the so-called American lifestyle of conspicuous consumerism, our planet would soon not be big enough to supply our needs, we would need four earths in order to support us. On the other hand, if everyone on earth lived a European lifestyle, we would need just two planet earths!

———————

However, we have just one earth and must take care to conserve its resources. Do not fall into the trap of conspicuous consumerism. Only buy what you need and make out a shopping list before you go to the supermarket. It will help you to avoid impulse purchases, which account for up to 70 per cent of what we buy.

Landmannalaugar, Iceland

Lifestyle – Start a toy library.

Too many children never have the opportunity to experience a normal childhood. More than 300,000 young boys worldwide are enlisted as child soldiers. Many are not even 10 years old. A total of 352 million children aged between 5 and 17 are forced to work; more than 246 million of these illegally, and almost 171 million under dangerous conditions.

———

In order to teach your children that there are alternatives to buying new toys, set up a toy library with friends. The variety of shared toys will certainly entertain the kids, and the toys will be used by more than one child, thereby reducing the number of toys that have to be produced.

Ice floes, Iceland

Leisure – Choose environmentally friendly holidays and outings.

Sustainable tourism attempts to make as small an impact on the environment and local culture as possible, while attempting to generate sustainable income and employment for local people. It seeks to be both ecologically and culturally sensitive. Ecotourism is the fastest growing sector of the world tourism industry.

If today's children are to become tomorrow's informed and responsible decision-makers, it is essential to help them become environmentally aware now. The next time you plan a family outing or holiday, chose an eco-friendly option.

Ibis, Venezuela

Biodiversity – Do not buy items made from turtle shell.

The illegal trade in wild animals is the greatest threat to their survival after the destruction of their habitat. Many traffickers deal in products that, by weight, are more valuable than cocaine or heroin. For example, a shawl made from shahtoosh, the extremely fine wool of the Tibetan antelope (which is on the verge of extinction), could be sold for more than US$15,000. Having inhabited world's oceans for millions of years, turtles are now in danger of extinction as a result of poaching.

If you are offered turtle shells or stuffed turtles when abroad, or other items made from their shells such as jewellery, combs, glasses frames, or trinkets, refuse to buy them.

Green turtle, Australia

Water – Use a bucket not a hose when you wash the car.

More than a billion people in the world (20 per cent of the population) cannot quench their thirst by drinking a glass of clean water. In certain countries, this is an extremely rare luxury. Only 30 per cent of the population of Cambodia, 27 per cent in Chad, 24 per cent in Ethiopia and 13 per cent in Afghanistan have access to clean water.

When you wash your car with a hose, 38 litres of drinking water are used every minute. It is better to use a few bucketfuls and a sponge. You will achieve the same result, but use far less water. If you insist on using a commercial car wash, which uses 32 to 150 litres of water per car, look for one that recycles its dirty water.

Lake Magadi, Kenya

Leisure – Take holidays in the country.

If you are looking for holiday accommodation that offers quick and easy access to the countryside, make use of the many hostels that are dotted around the UK. Often located in or close to areas of outstanding natural beauty, they normally offer good value for money.

──────────

Make sure you are armed with binoculars, field guides and maps to get the most out of your stay and make it enjoyable. Advice on what to look for locally can be obtained from tourist and information centres.

Ruwenzori mountains, Uganda

Consumption – Buy products that are free of genetically modified ingredients.

In 2003, around 167 million acres grown by 7 million farmers in 18 countries were planted with crops that had been genetically modified (GM) in some way. The most common transgenic features that resulted from the GM process were herbicide- and insecticide-resistance. In that same year, the United States grew 63 per cent of the world's genetically modified crops, while Canada grew just 6 per cent, but there were no GM crops grown commercially in the UK. Pro-GM groups claim that their products are more efficient and environmentally friendly; anti-GM groups argue that too little is known about the effect of GM foods on the environment and that multinational biotech groups are the only people who stand to gain anything. Currently, 5 companies control all GM crops in the world, with Monsanto producing 90 per cent of them.

Until the societal and environmental effects of genetically modified foods are known, try to limit the amount of GM food that you buy. Look for 'No GM' or 'GM free' labels.

Cranberries, United States

Transport – Take the train rather than the plane.

Every year, aviation generates as much carbon dioxide (which is largely responsible for climate change) as all the countries in Africa added together (excluding aviation). But carbon dioxide emissions from the aircraft are not the only environmental concern, airports create millions of litres of polluted wastewater each year.

———————————

Avoid taking the plane for journeys of less than 450 kilometres. Trains or buses are generally the least polluting means of transport for such distances.

Depression, Tasmania

Transport – Start a public cycling scheme.

The bicycle has unique advantages for getting around town: it is clean, silent, compact, fast and economical. The city of Rennes in France has decided to make 200 bicycles available, free, to its citizens. Users must first obtain a magnetic card from the city council, giving them access to the bikes between 6am and 2pm. After use, they can be returned to any one of the 25 pick-up points provided all over the city. The scheme has been running since 1998 and has some 2,000 regular users.

If you think this is a good idea and would like to see it trialled in your town, get in touch with your local authority.

Sandstone, Chad

Forests – Be careful not start a forest fire – do not smoke in the woods.

In 1997, huge forest fires devastated almost 4.5 million hectares of forest in Indonesia. The amount of smoke to which the people in the area were exposed was the equivalent of smoking 1,600 cigarettes per day and resulted in 40,000 people being hospitalised. When trees burn they release carbon into the atmosphere (the carbon that they store when absorbing harmful carbon dioxide). The Indonesian forests released 3.3 billion tonnes of carbon dioxide (the chief greenhouse gas) into the atmosphere when they burned, the equivalent of three times Japan's annual carbon dioxide emissions. It is likely that the fires were started deliberately to clear land for agriculture and livestock.

Do not smoke when walking in woods and never throw cigarette ends out of your car window, even if you think you have stubbed them out.

Yellowstone National Park, United States

Waste – do not pour cooking oil down the sink.

A city of 100,000 people produces nearly 300,000 litres of dirty water every day. Before it can be returned to nature or put back into the water supply, it must be cleaned in a treatment plant.

————————

Avoid pouring oils used in food or cooking down the sink, such as vinaigrette, oil from tuna cans and oil used for frying. They form a film that interferes with the functioning of water treatment plants by suffocating the bacteria that remove pollution. Instead, put such oils to one side in a closed plastic container. Once it is full, dispose of the oil with other non-recyclable waste.

Sand, Mauritania

Energy – Most oil pollution in the oceans is the result of human activity on land, not tanker spills.

They may be the most dramatic, but oil spills at sea are just a tiny part of the oil pollution that damages our oceans. Over 50 per cent of the oil in the earth's oceans comes from residential and industrial discharges. We often hear about storm water runoff (bearing car engine oil from car parks and streets) polluting our rivers, but all rivers eventually flow into the sea. Compare this to oil spills, which account for just 5 per cent of the oil polluting our oceans.

Fix a leaky car right away, and never dump your used oil into a stormdrain.

Pink flamingoes, Kenya

augaust 9th

Waste – Take your old refrigerator to be recycled.

An ice core sample taken from an Antarctic ice sheet shows that the levels of heat-trapping greenhouse gases are higher now than at any time in the last 420,000 years. The heat that these gases trap will, among other problems, cause sea levels to rise by as much as a metre. The agents responsible include coolant gases such as Freon (a brand name of CFCs, or chlorofluorocarbons), which is contained in the cooling circuits of old refrigerators, freezers and air conditioners. These harmful gases are released into the atmosphere when old fridges and similar appliances are discarded or dumped. It is estimated that 2 million refrigerators are disposed of every year in the United Kingdom.

Take your old refrigerator to a facility where it will be dealt with properly, or contact your local authority to find out how to dispose of it correctly.

Namib Desert, Namibia

Waste – Say 'no' to individually packaged portions.

The UK was responsible for an estimated 9.3 million tonnes of waste packaging in 2001. Packaging serves a purpose, but much of it is superfluous. The packaging that consumers see is only part of the story; many goods are packed in large boxes padded with foam or bubble wrap for transportation to commercial outlets. If they are shipped from abroad, the boxes are often packed on wooden pallets which are wrapped in plastic. It all adds up to a lot of waste!

The fashion for pre-packed mini-portions is just a marketing ploy to make a product more attractive and convenient, but you can create your own mini-portions. Instead of buying individual portions of food for mid-morning snacks or children's meals, buy in bulk and prepare your own, packing them in reusable plastic containers and bottles. Explain what you are doing to your children and hopefully they will adopt the habit for the future.

Glacial corridor, Greenland

Waste — Buy in bulk where possible.

For every rubbish bin placed at the kerb, 71 rubbish bins of waste are created in the production, transport, and industrial processes used to convert raw materials into finished products and their packaging

———————————

Limiting the amount of waste for disposal inevitably involves reducing the volume of packaging. For cheeses, sliced meats, and grains, buy your food in bulk, by weight, or cut to your requirement, rather than in pre-packaged portions. You will be able to find the ingredients for your next meal in the store cupboard rather than having to go shopping every time you prepare a meal.

www.grrn.or

Bacteria, Kamchatka, Russia

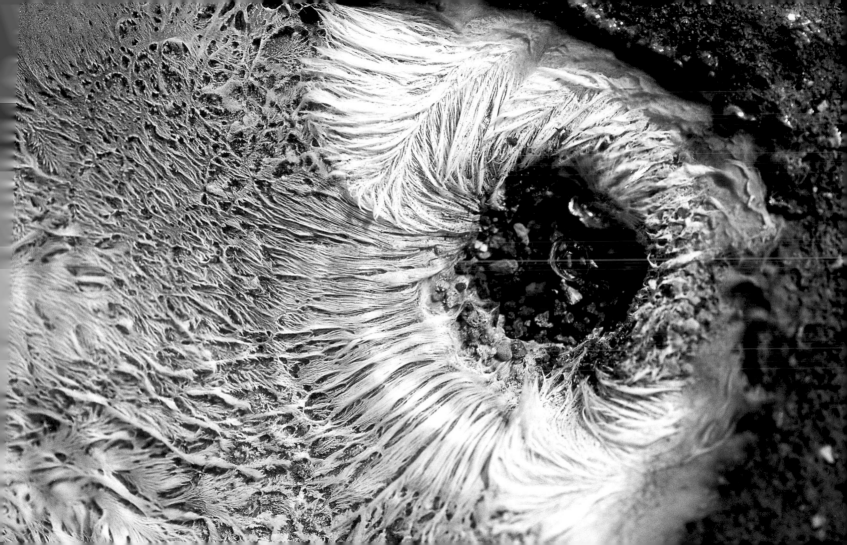

Noise – Be a good neighbour – mow the lawn at permitted times.

Try to keep noise down to an acceptable level at home and keep the peace with your neighbours at the same time. If work is being done on your house, make sure that the workmen observe local authority rules and only use loud equipment during the times permitted. A drill can produce between 90 and 100 decibels; the comfort threshold is 60 decibels.

We all contribute to the noise levels of our environment. Electrically-powered mowers or strimmers are very noisy. Do not use them at anti-social times. Could you revert to using a manual mower? In autumn, rake the leaves in your garden instead of using a leaf-blower. Enjoy the peace of your garden and listen to the sound of birdsong and the wind rustling in the leaves, rather than the sound of loud machinery.

Prairie, United States

Transport – Share your car and reduce pollution.

Natural disasters have worsened over the last 50 years. Human activity has disturbed natural habitats, reducing the land's ability to cushion the effects of sudden changes in weather. Natural disasters are also occurring more frequently, especially extreme weather events, which are becoming intense due to climate change. During the 1990s there were four times as many natural disasters as during the 1950s. These caused economic losses of about US$608 billion – more than the 4 previous decades put together.

Car sharing is one way of making environmentally friendly journeys. Use the Internet or intranet at work to find or offer car sharing facilities. Local universities and colleges often post notices about car sharing. Craigslist is a very effective way of matching people on the road (www.craigslist.org) and operates worldwide now. In the UK, some towns operate schemes in which certain road lanes can only be used by cars carrying more than one passenger during rush hour.

Lava, Kilauea volcano, Hawaii

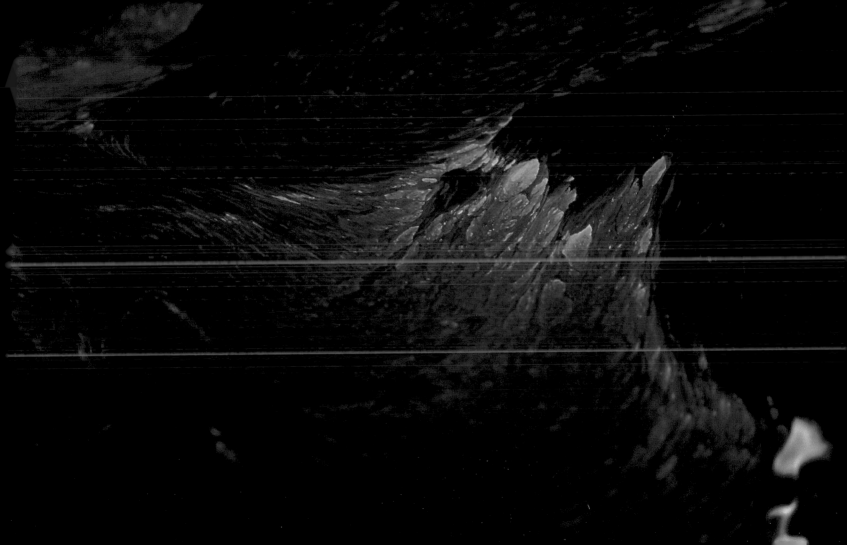

Leisure – When on holiday, look for labels indicating good environmental practices.

The European Eco-label identifies accommodation that complies with certain environmental criteria, such as water consumption, use of renewable energy resources, waste management and environmental education. The Eco-label encourages people who run tourist facilities to adopt good environmental practices and promotes sustainable tourism initiatives. Equivalent certification schemes exist on an international level as well.

Make being environmentally aware a priority when you go on holiday. Make use of accommodation and holiday facilities displaying these labels whenever you can.

Sandbanks, Mexico

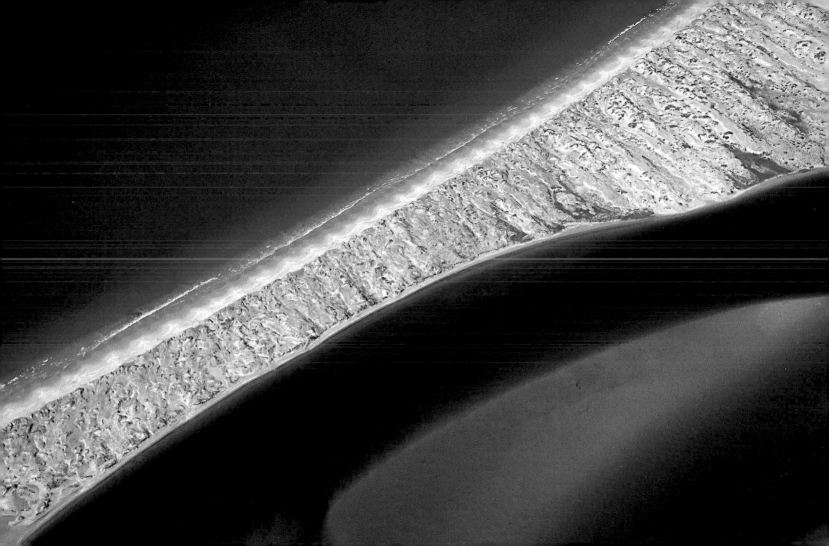

august 15th

Biodiversity – Help to clean up a river.

Local nature conservation associations regularly organise clean-up operations in rivers and streams. They remove any waste that is polluting the watercourse and clear banks of rubbish that has been discarded there. Vegetation that is excessively dense also needs to be cleared or thinned because it creates an enclosed habitat that is not beneficial for aquatic life. This kind of maintenance operation is therefore of use even if the water is not polluted, because it preserves the ecosystem and its biodiversity.

Clean-up operations always need volunteers. Take the plunge and join one. You will also learn more about rivers and streams and the animals and plants that live there.

Great Smoky Mountains, United States

august 16th

Forests – Take a walk in the forest with your children.

The earth's forests are home to an incalcuable number of animal and plant species. They act as a buffer against wind and retain rainwater, replenishing underground reserves. They also prevent soil erosion by retaining the soil and by absorbing the force of the rain as it falls. They absorb and store the carbon contained in carbon dioxide, giving off oxygen and helping to combat global warming (which is why they are referred to as carbon sinks). Wood is also the main source of energy for a third of the planet's inhabitants who do not have electricity. And every year, each of us in the developed world consumes the equivalent of 9 fully-grown trees in the form of paper.

While out walking in a forest or wooded environment with your children, explain to them its ecological function and some of the actions that they can take to safeguard it for the future.

River, Iceland

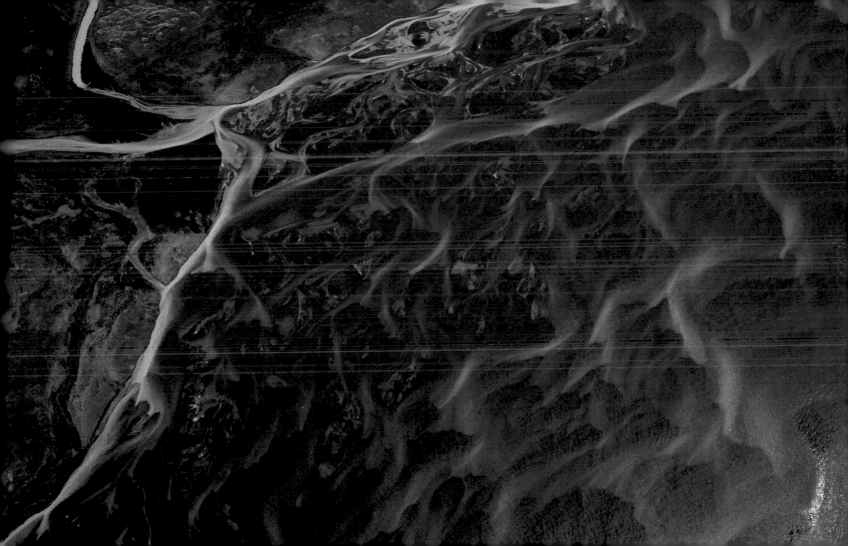

Energy – Choose mechanical over digital displays.

At present, a quarter of the world's population hogs three-quarters of the energy produced on the planet, while a third of the world does not even have electricity. For example, the United States consumes 22 times as much energy per inhabitant as India does. Part of the industrialised countries' energy consumption is due to gadgets and leisure equipment.

—————

If you are choosing between two different models of refrigerator, oven, or microwave, choose one with a mechanical display rather than one with a digital display, which is always switched on and so wastes energy.

Mehedjibat *erg* (sand desert), Algeria

The sea – Steer clear of Black Flag resorts when travelling around Europe.

The world's oceans play an important role in counteracting the effect of greenhouse gases: they are the biggest producer of oxygen (via plankton) and form the world's largest carbon sink (carbon is dissolved in water). Of the 7 billion tonnes of carbon dioxide that is produced by human activity every year, the sea absorbs 2 billion tonnes. By interacting with the atmosphere, the sea contributes to the climate and the formation of wind and clouds. Rich in fish, oil and mineral deposits (at depth under the seabed) and a source of energy (ocean currents and tides), the oceans are vitally important which is why it is essential that they remain clean and unpolluted.

___

Avoid resorts that have been given a Black Flag. This scheme is run by the European Surfrider Foundation, a non-profit organisation dedicated to the preservation of the coastal environment. The Black Flag indicates a polluted beach that poses a health risk.

Cuttlefish, Australia

Energy – Choose the most energy-efficient appliances.

Over 10 years, the difference between the cost of the electricity consumed by a highly energy-efficient refrigerator and by one that uses a lot of power can add up to 5 times the cost of a new refrigerator.

Check the European Energy rating label before you buy an electrical appliance. Refrigerators are especially of concern, since they are usually the biggest energy-consuming appliance in the home. Replace an old refrigerator with an A-rated model, and you will save enough energy to light the average household for almost 5 months.

Blizzard, Canada

Biodiversity – Avoid intrusive and noisy motorised activities.

Think about the impact on the environment and landscape of some leisure activities before you take part in them. Activities such as off-road driving, hunting, golf (the greens need considerable amounts of fertiliser and watering) and skiing (ski lifts, buildings and other structures required for the pistes) leave indelible marks on the landscape.

The people who take part in these activities should observe certain rules. For example, avoid using noisy motorised activities (such as jet skis, 4 x 4 vehicles, trail bikes and snowmobiles) outside the areas set aside for them, in order not to disturb plants and animals. Never drive an off-road vehicle on a beach, in a marsh, or anywhere else where birds nest.

Lake Titicaca, Bolivia

august 21st

Waste – Replace kitchen paper towels with a sponge.

The volume of waste we produce is increasing relentlessly. This is partly because people are ever more numerous, but also because each of us throws away more and more: as standards of living rise, more household waste is generated. In industrialised countries, each inhabitant produces 3 times as much waste as they did 20 years ago. The more the average income rises in developing countries, the more the global problem of waste will worsen. At the present rate, world production of waste is forecast to rise 70 per cent by 2020. And yet there are countless ways of reducing waste without damaging our standard of living.

———————————

In the kitchen, mop up spills with a sponge or cloth towel rather than a paper towel.

Grasses, Iceland

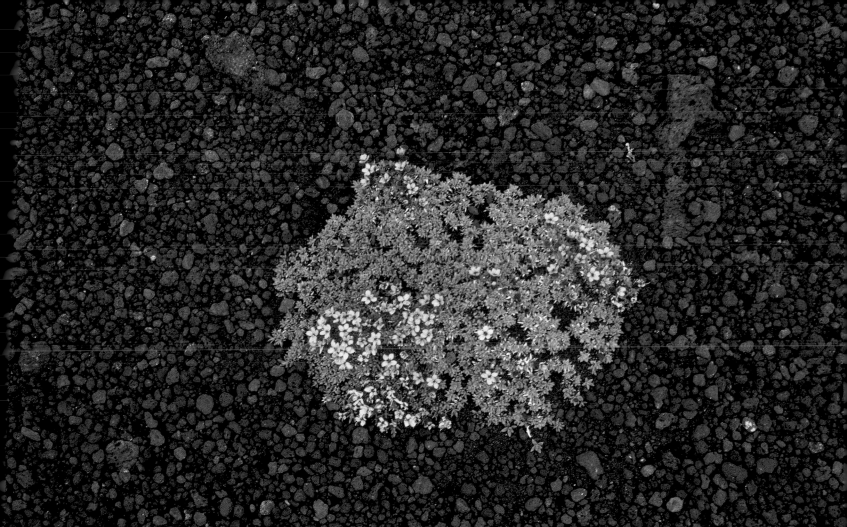

Forests – Choose FSC-certified wood for your furniture.

Half the world's tropical rainforests have disappeared over the last century. Examples of the uses to which their natural resources are put are all around us – from wooden furniture to insulation and from rope to medical treatments. The United States National Cancer Institute has identified 3,000 plants that are active against cancer cells, 70 per cent of which grow in the rainforest.

———————

Before buying any piece of furniture, ask where the materials come from, especially where exotic woods are concerned. Mahogany, teak, ipe and ebony are all examples of popular exotic woods. Choose sustainable products, such as FSC-certified products, from environmentally responsible companies that use resources without plundering nature or exploiting the local people.

Icebergs, Greenland

Agriculture – Buy Fair Trade coffee.

Fair Trade endeavours to put in place more equitable commercial relations between rich and poor countries, so that underprivileged workers and farmers can live and work with dignity. Workers on conventional farms are often required to meet harvesting quotas in order to receive their daily wage; workers bring their children to the plantation to help them make their quota. These children are technically not employees and thus are not protected by any laws. Fair Trade coffee eliminates the need for unfair quotas by stipulating that the coffee sells for a minimum of US$2.83 per kilogram. As a result, workers' earnings are unaffected by market fluctuations. In addition, Fair Trade coffee is usually grown on small farms, which cultivate under the rainforest canopy and without the use of pesticides.

Fair Trade coffee is now available in over 100 brands in over 35,000 markets worldwide. Make a commitment to only buy Fair Trade coffee, but if you can't do this at once, buy it as often as you can and work towards making Fair Trade products a normal part of your weekly shop.

Lake Titicaca, Bolivia

Energy – Cook with gas rather than electricity.

The 1,500 researchers of the United Nations' Intergovernmental Panel on Climate Change (IPCC), set up jointly by the UN Environment Program (UNEP) and the World Meteorological Organisation, now agree that human activity is affecting the world's climate. People cause more than 30 billion tonnes of greenhouse gases to be emitted in order to meet their energy needs in transport, heating, air conditioning, agriculture, industry, and so forth.

Pollution also occurs on a much smaller scale in our daily lives. A gas cooker uses, on average, half the energy of an electric one – as long as the burners are cleaned regularly. A clogged-up burner can use up to 10 per cent more energy than a clean one.

Nautilus, Australia

Waste – When travelling, take polluting waste home with you.

In some of the developing countries you visit, you might find that waste is neither disposed of nor treated, and it might not even be collected. Often such countries simply cannot afford to put in place the required infrastructure.

──────────

In order not to add to these countries' difficulties, take most of your polluting waste, such as plastic bags and batteries, home with you so that they can be disposed of correctly. On the other hand, you can probably leave tin cans behind with a clear conscience: local people are often skilled in the art of reusing them.

Scorpion fish, Australia

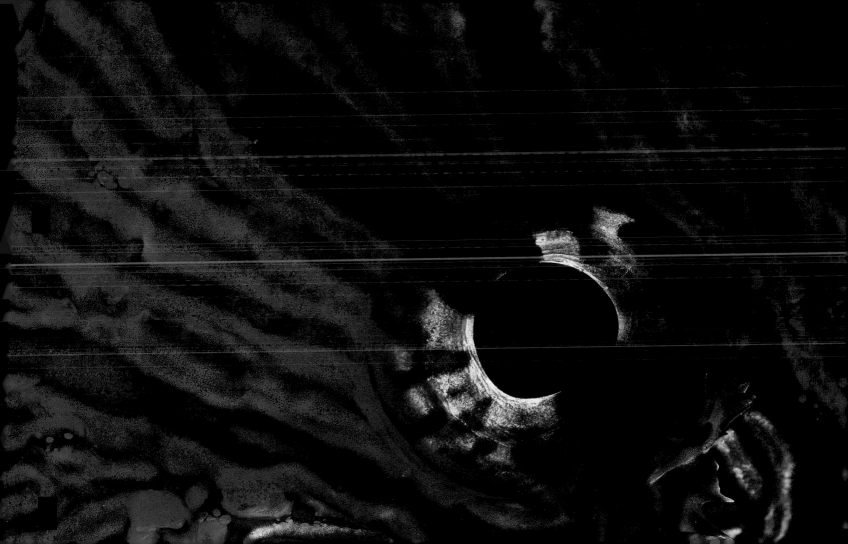

Coral reefs – Reduce your impact on global warming and save our coral reefs.

In the last few decades, more than 14 million hectares of coral reefs have been destroyed. A quarter of all marine life finds shelter in coral reefs. Now, thanks to climate change and the resulting increase in the temperature of the oceans, the algae that live within the coral tissue, providing it both with a source of food and its normal colour, are disappearing, sometimes leaving the coral bone white in a process called 'coral bleaching'. Deprived of its food supply, the coral can be killed by extensive bleaching.

———

The next time you are on holiday on a tropical beach, look at the wonders of the reef through different eyes. Make a mental link between these reefs and your everyday actions back at home. Try leaving your car in the garage as often as possible.

Coral reef, Australia

Waste – Buy products that can be refilled.

One quarter of the waste generated in the UK is due to packaging. By its very nature, packaging is disposable – you open the package, remove the product and discard the container.

Reducing the amount of packaging per product enables raw materials to be conserved, pollution to be reduced and needless transport to be avoided. To cut down on the amount of packaging that you throw away, choose products that are refillable – soap, liquid detergent, coffee, spices, rechargeable batteries, pens...

Ol Doinyo Lengaï volcano, Tanzania

Waste – Invest in a reusable filter for your coffeemaker.

On average, everyone in the United Kingdom throws out almost 500 kilograms of rubbish each year – the UK produced more than 30 million tonnes of household waste in 2002/2003. Managing this waste mountain, which is continuing to rise, is expensive in terms of land use, energy, pollution and time.

If you use disposable paper filters in your coffee machine, replace them with a reusable one made from cloth or stainless steel. As well as saving natural resources, the washable, reusable option is less expensive. As for the coffee grounds, rather than throwing them out along with other household waste, add them to your compost pile.

Maple, United States

Waste – Say 'no' to disposable nappies (1).

Disposable nappies are made from paper pulp, plastic and absorbent chemicals. Their manufacture requires 3.5 times as much energy, 8 times as much non-renewable raw material and 90 times as much renewable raw material as washable nappies. It also produces twice as much waste water. Disposable nappies produce 60 times as much waste as washable ones, and account for 4 per cent by volume of all waste. Each baby produces more than a tonne of dirty nappies, as landfill sites rapidly approach bursting point.

Using washable nappies daily for your child not only benefits the environment, it benefits your purse too, you could save over £1200.

Altiplano, Bolivia

Waste – Computers: a new environmental problem.

In the last 25 years, we have witnessed the birth and proliferation of the personal computer. Their lifespan is absurdly short – they are obsolete almost as soon as they are out of the box. A recent US study estimates that over 315 million computers became out-dated over the last 4 years. This represents a huge quantity of lead, plastic and other materials.

Although computers consume relatively little energy when they are in use, the combination of an intensive manufacturing process and short lifespan means that the total amount of energy that they use is roughly equal to that of a refrigerator, one of the most energy voracious of all home appliances.

Mudflats, Alaska

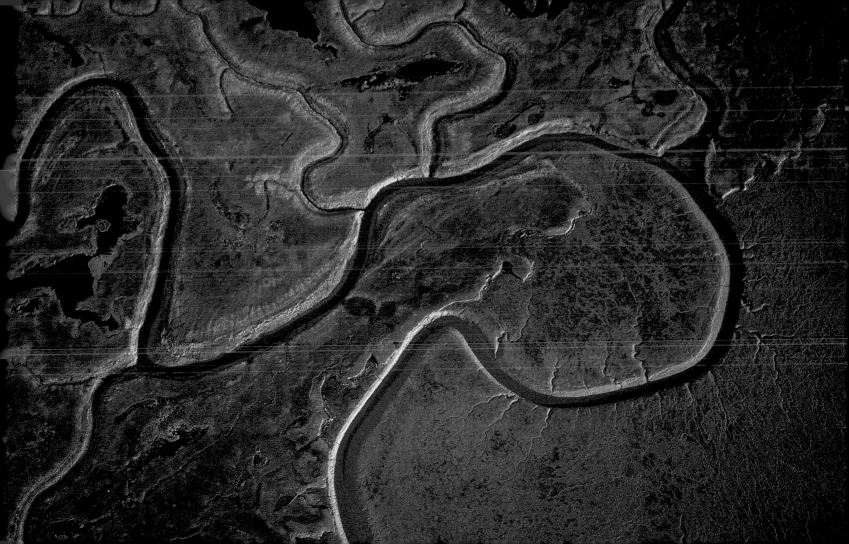

Transport of goods – When travelling, eat local food.

A study of the loss of tourism revenue in Thailand estimated that 70 per cent of the money spent by tourists eventually left the country through hotel chains, tour operators, airlines and the importation of food and drink. To counteract this trend, choose small, local hotels, local transport and services that earn money for local people, such as guides, cooks, mule- or donkey-drivers, porters and domestic servants.

When you are thousands of kilometres from home, be adventurous and try the local specialities (providing it is safe to do so, you should be careful of eating fresh fruit and vegetables in some countries). Those tasteless apples which have travelled half-way around the world, producing pollution in the process, will never taste as good as the local mangoes. Try local specialties, fruit, and vegetables and discover new dishes in the process.

Great Smoky Mountains, United States

The sea – If fishing is your sport, help to preserve fish stocks.

The depletion of the world's ocean fish stocks is due, among other things, to over-fishing on an international scale. The fish that are caught are frequently small since they have not had the time to grow to maturity, and if they are caught before they have been able to reproduce, their stocks cannot be replenished.

If fishing is your sport, make sure that you respect the size limit for whatever you catch and throw back any fish that are too small. When you go fishing on holiday, find out which species are restricted by contacting the port authority or by asking at a tourist office, and, if necessary, make sure your fellow fishermen are aware of the restrictions too. And finally, do not catch more than you need.

Shark, Australia

Waste – Consider rechargeable batteries.

An incredible 50 times as much energy is used to manufacture a battery, as the battery itself will produce during its life. The only exception is a rechargeable battery. A conventional battery in a personal stereo will last for around 6 days, but a rechargeable battery can be recharged numerous times. Like disposable batteries, some rechargeable batteries contain cadmium, but since they can be recharged between 400 and 1,000 times, their impact on the environment is reduced considerably – providing that they are disposed of correctly at the end of their life.

To reduce the ecological impact of batteries on the environment, choose those that contain neither mercury nor cadmium, but better still, choose rechargeable batteries. They are extremely economical to use – the initial cost of buying both batteries and charger will soon be recovered.

Mudflats, United States

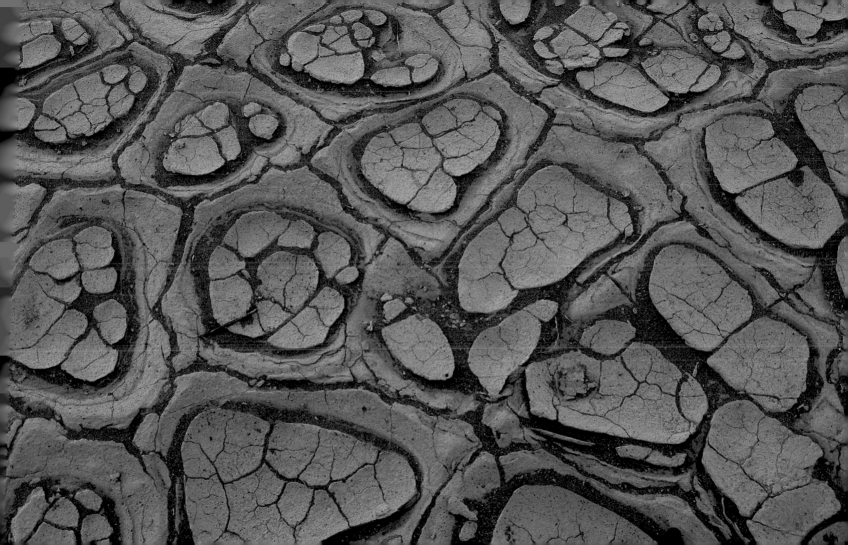

Transport – Reduce the number of school runs – take your children on foot.

Although there are 800 million vehicles in the world today (10 times as many as in 1950), 80 per cent of the world's inhabitants possess no car and travel by bus, bike, horse-drawn cart, or on foot. Cars already produce between a fifth and a third of all carbon dioxide emissions and their numbers are scheduled to increase considerably over the coming decades, to meet growing demand in developing countries. In the UK, just 20 years ago, one third of primary school-aged children made their way to school on their own. Now less than 10 per cent of children make their own way.

———————————

Instead of taking your children to school by car, send them by public transport or school bus, or accompany them on foot or by bike.

Bristlecone pine, United States

september 4th

Waste – Replace paper and plastic cups with regular cups and glasses.

Our lifestyle over the last 20 years has demanded far too much of the earth. Our use of natural resources exceeded the earth's natural capacity by 20 per cent in 2000; by 2050, it is expected that this figure will have risen to between 80 per cent and 120 per cent.

Many workplaces provide plastic cups for water and coffee. They are used for just a few minutes before being thrown away. To stop wasting several plastic cups a day, take your own cup to work and urge your colleagues to do the same. You will also be doing your company a favour, by saving them the cost of the disposable cups.

Yellowstone National Park, United States

Energy – Control your heating with a thermostat.

The energy used to heat the home is a huge drain on resources. However, the temperature can easily be regulated according to the way each room is used, how often it is occupied and taking into account how cold it is outside.

———

Installing a digital thermostat system allows you to set your heating room by room as required. You will be able to save up to a quarter more energy than if your heating were not regulated.

september 6th

Waste – Pick up one piece of rubbish each day.

Landfill remains the main method of waste disposal worldwide. In the United Kingdom, 111 million tonnes of household, commercial and industrial waste are disposed of in this way each year. Decomposing rubbish in landfill sites produces a third of the methane emissions that contribute to global warming. Apart from their foul smell, landfill sites also contaminate water because not all landfills are equipped with barriers to prevent pollutants from spreading.

Even our everyday surroundings are not free from rubbish. If each of us bent down once a day to pick up a piece of waste, 290 million pieces of rubbish would be removed from the streets and pavement every day.

Prairie, Mount Rainier, United States

Biodiversity – Follow the rules in protected areas.

Worldwide, about 34,000 plant species, or a quarter of the total species of flora on the planet, face extinction in the coming years. In the UK, close to 200 plant species have been identified as being threatened with extinction; some exist only in botanical gardens, having already become extinct in the wild. Other plants enjoy the security of growing within the boundaries of a national park, but this protection is only effective if visitors observe the rules.

Read the instructions displayed at the entrance to parks – they are there for a reason. By keeping your dog on a lead, you will not disturb the wildlife and by following the marked trails you will not tread inadvertently on protected plants.
www.defra.gov.uk/

Pink flamingoes, Kenya

Noise – Soundproof floors to avoid disturbing the neighbours.

A recent British research paper found that 21 per cent of people questioned felt their home lives were being disrupted by noise, while twice as many of those who replied felt irritated by noise from the road.

———————

If you live in a flat and have people beneath you, carpeting is the best way to soundproof the floor. If you have a tiled or hardwood floor, put castors under the feet of furniture to help reduce the scraping sounds caused when it is moved; place electrical appliances on shock-absorbing pads to reduce the amount of vibration transmitted through the floor, and lay rugs in strategic places to dampen the sound of footsteps.

Crater Lake, United States

Consumption – Borrow or lend your power tools.

The use of power tools is sometimes necessary for solid, reliable craftsmanship. But often, homeowners invest in these tools without considering how frequently they will be used. How many hours each year will you use an electric drill? What about a power saw, high-pressure heat gun, concrete mixer, or carpet shampoo machine? Our cupboards and garages are cluttered with equipment and tools that we use only very rarely, if at all.

Rather than investing in new tools, why not try another approach? How about borrowing them from a neighbour or family member, or buying them jointly and taking turns using them? Consider starting a tool-sharing programme in your neighbourhood. Find out what people's needs and interests are, it's a great way to build a sense of community.

Tree bark, United States

Transport – Try car sharing.

Carbon dioxide is one of the main greenhouse gases responsible for global warming. In the 1780s, just before the Industrial Revolution, carbon-dioxide levels were stable at around 280 parts per million (PPM). Scientists can tell this by measuring the levels remaining in ice core samples from the time. By 1930, levels were up to 315 PPM; by the 1970s they had reached 330 PPM. In the mid 1990s, levels measured 360 PPM and in the past decade they have risen by 20 PPM. The world is rapidly becoming warmer and the proliferation of cars plays a key role in this.

In metropolitan areas in some European countries, car-sharing programmes have gained a lot of popularity over the last few years. A magnetic card gives you access to a fleet of vehicles that can be picked up at various points in the city and you pay according to how long you use them and how far you travel. Someone else worries about the maintenance and extra costs. All you need to do is get in and drive off.

Red ibis, Venezuela

Agriculture – Replace meat protein with protein from other sources.

The world's greatest tropical forest, the majestic Amazon rainforest, is retreating hour by hour before the onslaught of chainsaws, which have already cut down 15 per cent of its original area. Over the last 30 years, 40 per cent of the cleared Amazon rainforest land has been converted to cattle grazing. The export of beef benefits only a minority of the local population, while a quarter of Brazil's population lives in poverty, on less than US$1 a day.

The frequent consumption of meat by citizens of wealthy countries is a recent phenomenon. Yet, it is harmful to health, increasing the risk of heart attack and obesity. Replace meat with vegetable protein, such as soya, pulses, and nuts. Cooked soya beans are the best source of vegetable protein; when boiled and salted, soya beans also make a delicious snack.

Sandstone, Chad

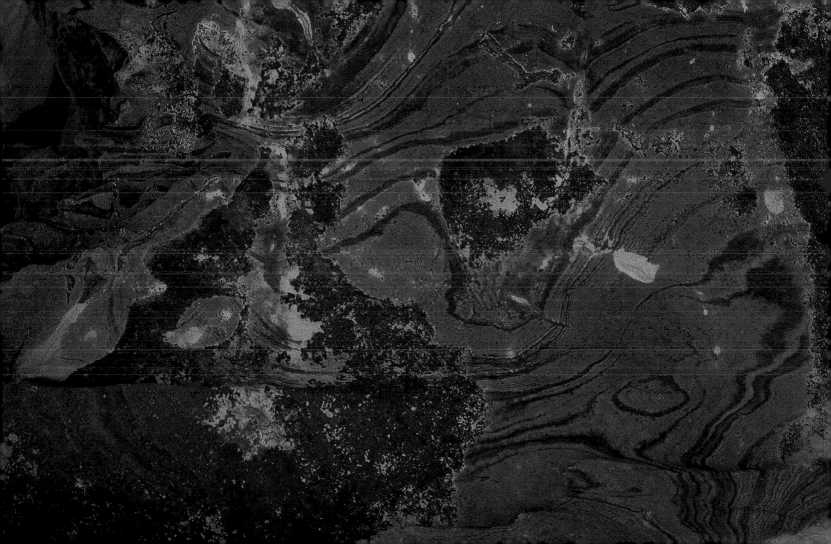

Gardening – Do not use chemicals close to water.

A garden is a field in miniature, but even on this small scale, it is essential not to contribute to water and soil pollution by using too many chemicals. American gardeners use 30 million kilograms of lawn pesticides every year. Homeowners apply 3.5 to 11 kilograms of lawn pesticides per hectare, while agricultural land is generally treated with 3 kilograms of pesticides per hectare.

——————————

Do not use fertiliser, pesticides or herbicides near any body of water such as a well, stream, pool, or marsh. Each time these products are used, they soak into the soil, sometimes polluting aquifers permanently.

Emperor penguins, Antarctica

Lifestyle – Adopt a pet from your local animal shelter or rescue centre.

According to Dogs Trust, the largest UK dog welfare charity, over 100,000 stray dogs were collected last year. By adopting at dog or cat from a rescue centre, you are giving a homeless animal a new chance in life. The Cat's Protection League is the UK's largest and oldest feline charity. It rescues and rehomes abandoned and unwanted cats and promotes responsible cat ownership.

___

If you would like to give a home to an animal, contact the Royal Society for the Prevention of Cruelty to Animals (RSPCA), who will also give advice on care, or visit your local animal shelter. By buying an animal from a shop, you are encouraging even more animals to be raised as pets.

Bear track, Russia

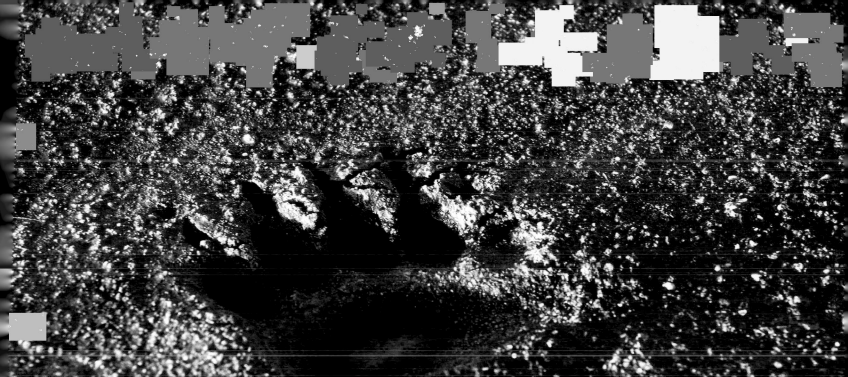

Energy – Choose the right light bulbs.

Energy-saving measures need not be constraining or austere – just a small change can make a big difference. To make your lighting more environmentally friendly, check the light bulbs you are using. The powerful light of a 100-watt bulb does not suit a bedroom or a room that is naturally bright. During the course of a year, a halogen lamp consumes as much energy as two washing machines. Redirect wall lights to light the ceiling, from where the light will be bounced back, or use uplighters. Think about installing neon lights in the garage, which are as energy-efficient as compact fluorescent light bulbs.

If you are planning to do some decorating at home, remember that light-coloured walls make the best use of light and require less artificial lighting.

Dunes, Libya

Waste – Use the Internet to look up telephone numbers.

New telephone directories are issued each year and often consist of several volumes if covering a heavily populated area. The Yellow Pages Directory offers a free hotline on where and how to recycle old directories. But while recycling them is much better than throwing them away, it is even better not to have them in the first place – remember, putting something in a recycling bin, while always better than the waste bin, still results in the use of an energy resource of some kind in order to carry out the recycling.

How many times have you looked in the telephone directory this year? If you do not use it, ask not to receive it. Use the Internet to look up phone numbers instead (both national and international). If you are off on your travels, the Internet is also a good place to find mapping and route planners.

Niger River, Mali

september 16th

Lifestyle – Introduce environmental education to schools.

Many local environmental non-profit organisations offer free, or low-cost, educational presentations or field trips for school-aged children; often it is simply a matter of asking. They focus on the environmental problems faced by your area or offer tours of the natural features it has to offer.

If you would like environmental education to be a higher priority in your children's education, spend some time investigating the organisations offering such educational resources. It is a good way to increase awareness among students, their teachers and other parents.

Puffin, Round Island, Alaska

Forests – Plant a tree.

Thousands of years ago, when man first settled and began to grow crops, half the earth's land mass was covered in thick forest. Today, less than a third is still forested. Over the last 10 years, forest cover has diminished by 2.4 per cent worldwide. All plants release oxygen and absorb carbon dioxide in order to survive and in so doing help cleanse the atmosphere. A hectare of mature forest absorbs the equivalent of a year's worth of carbon dioxide emissions from 250 cars.

Plant a tree and join in the fight against global warming and atmospheric pollution caused by carbon dioxide emissions.

Lassen National Park, United States

Chemicals – Use white wine vinegar to remove lime scale.

Heavy metals (mercury in batteries, lead in gasoline) and oil-based pollutants (especially plastic in its innumerable forms) are among the most harmful products. When they penetrate the atmosphere or enter soil and water, they contaminate the entire food chain up to and including people. In Europe and the United States, testicular cancer rates have tripled over half a century, and one woman in 8 now develops breast cancer, as compared to one in 20 in 1960.

───────────

Chemical compounds are in widespread use in farming, but they also feature in the household cleaners that have invaded our home. In some cases they are unnecessary, another, less toxic substance would do just as well. To remove lime scale from tiles, taps, kettles and irons, just use white wine vinegar.

Crater Lake National Park, United States

Biodiversity – Keep rural areas rural.

Wild places are constantly being gobbled up by urban development – each year 6,500 hectares of land is converted from rural to urban use by the construction industry. The development of natural habitats is the biggest cause of the loss of biodiversity in the world.

Live as close to where you work as possible. Use public transport alternatives and discover the joys of living in a vibrant, urban neighbourhood.

Indian summer, Canada

september 20th

Waste – Sustainable equipment for school.

The return to school in the autumn gives parents the chance to make sure that their children are equipped for the classroom with items made from sustainable or recyclable resources. Much of the budget will be spent on paper products.

——————

Choose rulers and pencil sharpeners made of metal or wood (but not coloured or varnished), which will last longer than their plastic equivalents and produce less pollution when thrown away. Choose a solar-powered calculator, rather than a battery-powered one. Buy folders and exercise books made from recycled paper, but also sift through last year's stationery to see what can be reused. Encourage your children to trade supplies with friends to foster the habit of reuse.

Um el Ma lake, Libya

Energy – Avoid washing at too high a temperature.

If we reduce the amount of energy used in the home for domestic purposes such as lighting, heating and cooking, we reduce the overall demand for energy. As a result, power stations are required to produce less electricity, leading to a reduction in atmospheric pollution.

Energy savings are possible wherever we look, even in the laundry. Thanks to the new washing powders, clothes can be washed effectively at 30°C, there is little need to use the very hot 90°C wash – a wash cycle at 40° consumes 3 times less electricity than one at 90°C.

Adélie penguins, Antarctica

Waste – Buy remoulded (retreaded) tyres.

Every year, some 281 million tyres are scrapped. Of this quantity, 42 per cent are used for fuel (to provide energy) and 26 per cent are recycled to make material that can be used in industry. In total, in some form or other, 8 out of every 10 tyres finds a new use. Despite this, over 300 million old tyres lie stockpiled, creating hiding places for rats and other vermin and causing air and water pollution around the stockpiles.

It takes half as much energy to remould an old tyre as to make a new one. To encourage this practice, which is both economical and environmentally friendly, choose remoulds.

Silversword, Hawaii

Water – Choose household appliances that use less water.

With increased wealth comes increased water use. When people have more disposable income they are likely to buy more consumer and household goods, resulting in higher water use. Increased purchasing power also means that more goods are likely to be bought that use water in their production. More water is used in the production of paper, for example, than in any other material. Metal and steel works alone account for 20 per cent of the water used by industry.

Washing machines and dishwashers use a considerable amount of water. Always use them on full load, or use the half load button. If you are buying a new machine, look for a label indicating water efficiency.

Barracudas, Australia

september 24th

Waste – Recycle plastic.

Most plastic bottles today are made of polyethylene terephthalate (PET), which is recyclable.
The PET symbol, which is marked on the bottom of plastic containers, consists of a triangle of arrows surrounding the number 1. Plastic packaging which has been sorted and recycled is reborn in many different ways: fleece garments, watering cans, flower pots, floor coverings, water bottles, carpets, car parts, phone cards... Each tonne of recycled plastic saves the energy equivalent of 11 barrels of oil.

At home, in the office, or when travelling, be sure to recycle plastic drink bottles. If your office does not have a recycling programme, encourage them to start. Recycling a single plastic bottle saves enough energy to keep a 60-watt bulb alight for 6 hours.

Mount Pinatubo, Philippines

Lifestyle – Take an active part in important environmental discussions.

As part of our daily lives, we attend meetings and discuss issues that can have a big impact on the environment – such as a meeting to discuss the site proposed for a new supermarket, or the disposal of waste in a block of flats.

———————

Every issue of this kind can contribute to preserving the world's natural resources, limiting pollution and reducing energy waste. Make your feelings known and speak out in defence of environmental measures, such as eco-friendly heating, the sorting and recycling of waste, the low-energy lighting of communal areas, the creation of green spaces or shared gardens. Help your colleagues to become aware of the environmental issues at stake.

Wreck, Mexico

The sea – Ask your fishmonger about the origins of the fish he sells.

The world's fishing industry has undergone a real revolution during the last 50 years: giant nets, fleets of factory ships with radar to detect shoals of fish, and international treaties mapping out fishing boundaries (that often include waters off poor countries, where the income from fishing is of great importance). The result is that today 90 million tonnes of fish are caught every year, compared with 20 million tonnes caught in 1950. By 2010, based on projected population growth, the demand for fish could rise to 120 million tonnes a year. This is extremely worrying, given that the level of fishing is already too high to enable stocks to recover naturally: 11 of the world's great fishing grounds are being progressively depleted.

Ask your fishmonger about the problem of over-fishing and where his stock comes from.

Crabs, Galapagos Islands

Lifestyle – You have the power to vote, in more ways than one!

Voting gives the ordinary citizen the power to have a say in who runs the country. The people in government should, in theory, set an example. Find out about the environmental policies of the various political parties and vote accordingly.

Do not forget that you also vote several times per day, by making choices as a consumer. These choices can be just as influential in instigating changes in the way goods are manufactured and how society and the economy are organised.

Moose, Alaska

Waste – Recycle magazines and newspapers.

Approximately 20 per cent of household rubbish consists of paper and card, including newspapers and magazines. This is equal to over 4 kilograms of waste paper per UK household each week.

————————

Recycle your used paper and card. It will be used to make new paper, as well as items such as egg cartons, packaging, tissues, paper napkins and tablecloths and toilet paper. Give old magazines to friends, or offer them to the waiting room of your local laundrette, dentist, or hairdresser, where they will be read over and over.

Maui island, Hawaii

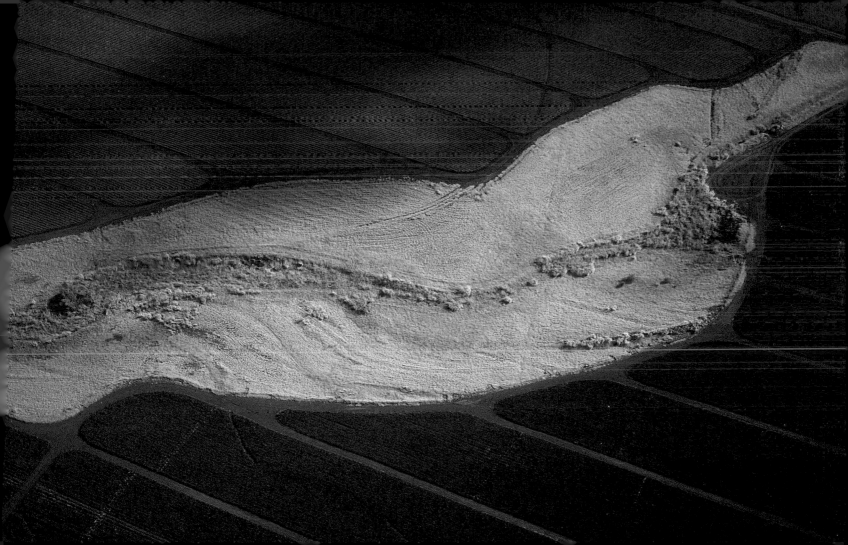

september 29th

Consumption – Look for eco-labels and choose those products when possible.

The European Eco-label – a small blue and green flower with 12 stars for petals – has been in existence since 1992. It enables consumers to identify products that have less impact on the environment because they use fewer natural resources (raw materials, water, and energy) in their manufacture, are less damaging when used, and produce little or no waste when they are discarded (i.e. they can be recycled). By choosing products that are approved consumers preserve the environment and encourage manufacturers to come up with even more environmentally friendly products. Eco-labels are only of value when the organisation certifying the producers is independent. Make sure that the organisation certifying the labels is not linked in any way to any of the producers.

Be a careful and caring consumer. Do your homework and scrutinise those labels before you buy. It will benefit both you and the environment.

Kap Farvel region, Greenland

Energy – Switch off the iron when there is just one garment left to press.

Though the market for renewable energy continues to be just a fraction of the entire energy market, it is beginning to grow. Solar-powered technologies have matured greatly since they first appeared. The sun's power can now be harnessed and converted to electricity via photovoltaic (PV) systems (solar panels).

———————————

All the small changes that we make to our energy consumption will, particularly if we make a habit of them, make a difference to the world. At home, when only one or two garments remain to be pressed, unplug the iron – the residual heat in the iron should be sufficient to finish the job, particularly for those garments that do not require the hottest setting. Every little helps!

Tassili du Hoggar, Algeria

Energy – Have your windows fitted with double-glazing.

Most air pollution comes from road transport (nitrogen dioxide and carbon monoxide), industry (sulphur dioxide, which produces acid rain), and domestic heating (carbon monoxide). These can damage human health (by causing breathing problems, migraines and lesions) as well as the environment. Some of these polluting gases contribute to increasing the greenhouse effect.

To reduce your consumption of energy for heating and the polluting emissions that are produced, why not install double-glazing. It insulates against heat loss and against noise. If you cannot afford double-glazing, remember to close all the curtains at night.

Thaw, Greenland

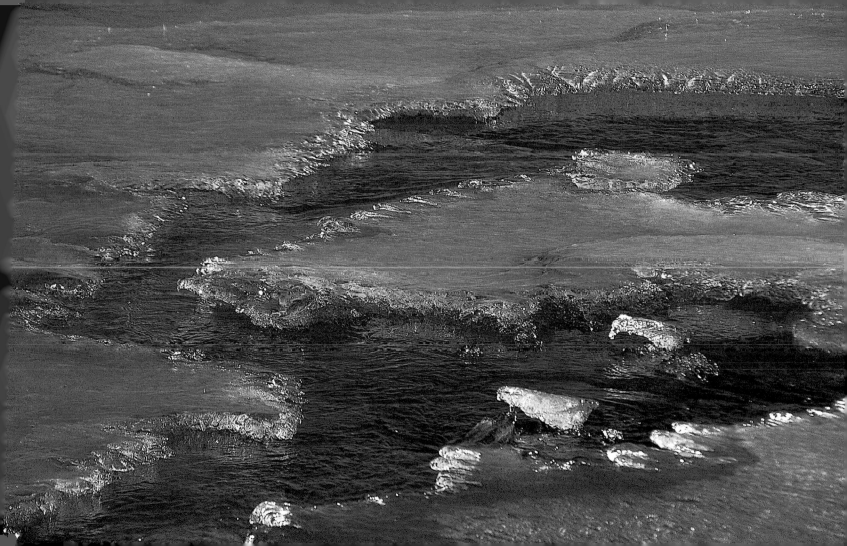

Transport – Use a car-sharing scheme.

If we do not succeed in curbing the changes that the climate is undergoing thanks to our activities and contemporary lifestyle, tomorrow's climate will be quite different. Various signs of this can be observed already. Since 1989, Mount Kilimanjaro has lost a third of its snow and could be completely bare within 15 years. The spring ice thaw in the Northern Hemisphere takes place 9 days earlier than it did 150 years ago and the first freeze of autumn occurs 10 days later than previously. This has dramatic effects on bird migration and crop production.

Over the last 20 years, traffic has increased by 70 per cent on roads in the UK. Suggest car sharing with your neighbours or colleagues; your fuel consumption will be reduced, along with wear on your car, you will take up less road space and help to combat global warming.

Sandstone, Chad

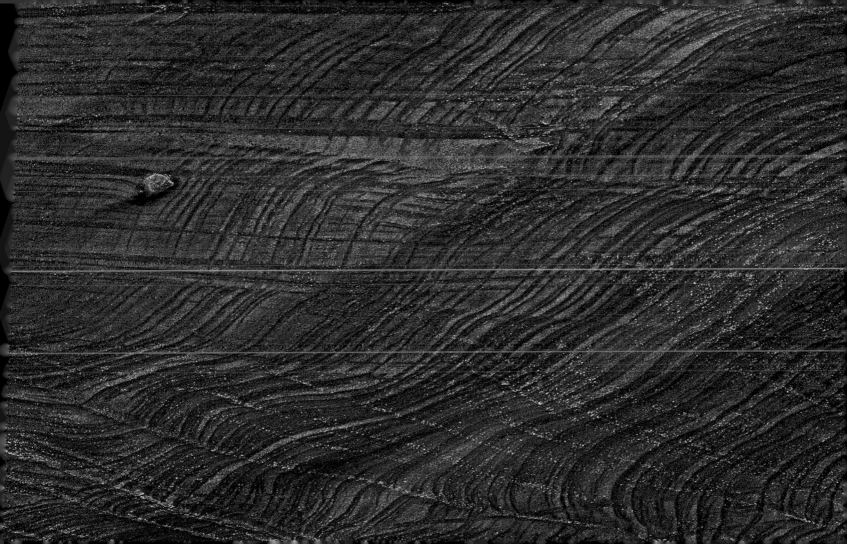

october 3rd

Waste – Reject junk mail to reduce the volume of waste.

We produce ever-greater quantities of waste. Our letterboxes are clogged with catalogues and advertising: British households receive 4 billion pieces of direct mail each year. This mail, one-third of which goes directly into the dustbin, swells the volume of household waste, increasing the cost of collecting and treating it.

————————————

When dealing with a company or organisation that knows your address, always tell them to keep it private. This will prevent them from selling it to other organisations with a mailing list. Contact the Mailing Preference Service (www.mpsonline.org.uk), and request to have your name removed from mailing lists.

Fjord, southern Greenland

The sea – Report any signs of pollution immediately.

Around 2,500 species of fish, shellfish and other sea life are exploited commercially worldwide. Over-fishing by well-equipped and excessively large fishing fleets is already reducing fish stocks considerably and the pollution of the sea is only adding to the problem. Over-fishing and pollution could have severe effects on world food supplies, especially in developing countries, where one billion people depend on fish for food.

If you notice any apparent signs of pollution in freshwater, such as froth, a brown residue, or the smell of sewage, alert your regional or town water authority. If you notice any pollution while at the beach, such as waste or oil, notify the relevant authority at once.

Scorpion fish, Australia

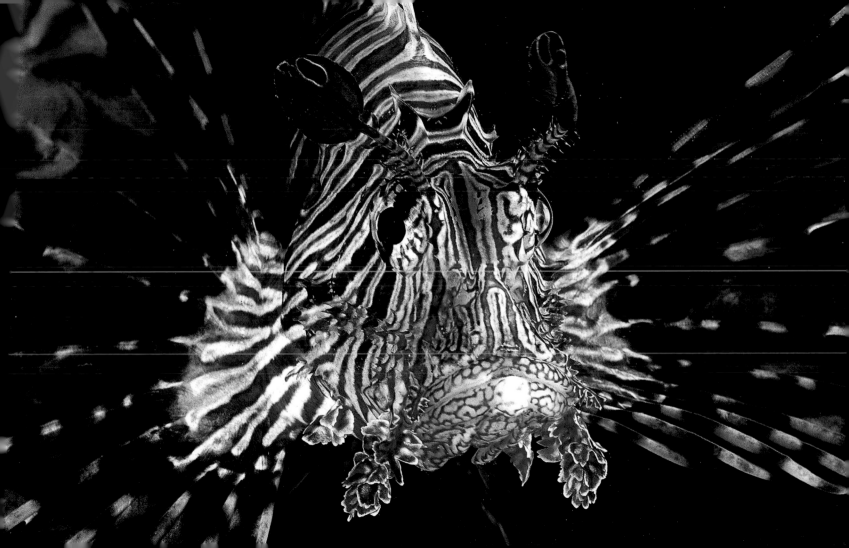

october 5th

Waste – Buy recycled paper.

Recycling paper, while important, is only one part of the lifecycle of paper. We must also look at paper consumption. Recycled paper is widely available now and is considerably less damaging to the environment in its production. Every tonne of paper that is recycled saves 30,000 litres of water, 3000-4000 kWh of electricity, and produces 95 per cent less air pollution.

————————————

Choose paper, box files, folders, envelopes, cards, toilet paper, and paper towels made from recycled paper and cardboard.

Northern forest, Finland

Chemicals – Do not use air fresheners sold as aerosols.

Chlorofluorocarbons (CFCs), which first appeared in the 1930s, are used chiefly in refrigerators, aerosol canisters and fire extinguishers. They are now known to be responsible for about 80 per cent of the damage to the ozone layer, the atmospheric layer that protects us from the sun's damaging ultra-violet rays. One molecule of CFC can destroy up to 100,000 molecules of ozone and, since the 1970s, the concentration of CFCs in the atmosphere has risen by 20 per cent.

Disregarding, for a moment, the pollution caused by CFCs, air fresheners sold in aerosol cans are also toxic, flammable and produce waste. Replace them with more environmentally friendly potpourris, essential oil diffusers, candles, incense, fragrant plants (jasmin or gardenia), citrus fruit peel, or oranges studded with cloves.

Krakatau volcano, Indonesia

Waste – Use reusable carrier bags.

Each year, United Kingdom supermarkets provide customers with 17.5 billion plastic carrier bags. If left to decompose, a plastic bag will take 200 years. If incinerated, it produces pollution. In the sea, plastic bags prove fatal for some sea creatures, which swallow them, mistaking them for jellyfish, and they are not biodegradable in salt water. As many as 46 thousand pieces of plastic contaminate each square mile of ocean.

When you visit the supermarket, bring reusable bags, and rediscover your trusty old shopping bags and baskets. Keep your bags on a hook by the front door so you can always grab them on your way out to the shops.

Humpbacked whale, Polynesia

Chemicals – Support the requirements of the Basel Convention.

The Basel Convention, which came into force in 1992, provides an effective legal framework for controlling and reducing cross-border movements of dangerous waste. It was drawn up by 152 states and, in 2002, led to the issuing of a list of 12 chemical products declared to be persistent organic pollutants (POPs), whose manufacture and use are now prohibited. Among wood treatments, the most toxic, such as arsenic, have been banned, but those that have replaced them are not without dangers of their own.

Learn about the hazardous waste trade and what you can do to prevent it. Use natural products such as beeswax and linseed oil to protect your wood.

Mount Rainier National Park, United States

Water – Find out what happens to your waste water.

Water is the source of all life. We depend upon it completely. It is also the chief constituent of all living things: 65 per cent of our bodies and 75 per cent of our brains are water. It plays a part in economic life, allowing the irrigation of cultivated land, the manufacture of industrial products and the production of electricity. It also provides superb leisure facilities. It is irreplaceable, guaranteeing hygiene and the comfort of our day-to-day lives.

Once water has been used and is dirty, it vanishes down the drain, but where does it go from there? Contact your local authority and find out. Ask what happens at your local treatment plant. Once water is out of sight it should not be out of mind. By taking an interest in how dirty water is recycled, you will be helping to keep the water companies on their toes.

Glacier, Greenland

Waste – Say 'no' to disposable nappies (2).

It takes 4.5 trees to produce the pulp required to make the 4,600 disposable nappies needed to keep the average baby clean and dry, and a glassful of crude oil to make the protective plastic layer found in just one disposable nappy. Although a disposable nappy is only worn for a few hours before being thrown away, it will take around 400 years to decompose in a landfill site. There is an alternative: washable towelling nappies. Absorbent, effective and comfortable, the modern towelling nappy is shaped for ease of use and very different from the towelling nappy of years ago.

Since 8 million disposable nappies are thrown away every day in the UK, choose the economical and environmentally friendly option and cover your baby's bottom in a towelling nappy.

Forests in the Ruwenzori massif, Uganda

Waste – Give unused medicines to a humanitarian organisation.

In developing countries, 30,000 people die every day for lack of medicines or the money to buy them. In the West, meanwhile, we throw unused medicines out with the household rubbish. Humanitarian organisations collect and redistribute medicines to those in need around the world. In 2003, 510 tonnes, or the equivalent of 20 million boxes, were redistributed.

Find a non-profit organisation that accepts unused medicines. It will reduce the amount of medicine lying around your house that could fall into a young child's hands – 40 per cent of poisoning cases involving children are the result of swallowing medicines not intended for them.

Indian summer, United States

Energy – Use the sleeper timer.

Scientists say that the web of habitats, natural resources and species that makes up life on earth will only be able to adapt, in the coming years, to a presumed average temperature increase of 0.1°C and a 2 centimetre rise in sea levels. To remain within these limits, worldwide greenhouse gas emissions would have to be cut by 60 per cent at once. This is impossible. The faster warming takes place, the more difficult it will be to control its consequences. Hence, the need for immediate action.

Televisions and stereos often have sleep timers, which shut off the appliance after a given amount of time. If you normally fall asleep watching television or listening to music, this will allow you to do so without wasting energy by allowing the appliance to run all night.

Mount Adams volcano, United States

Waste – Print on both sides of the paper.

Forests are exploited to produce wood on an industrial scale. This wood is used for building, carpentry and the manufacture of paper and card. The paper industry uses 40 per cent of commercially produced wood, however, 17 per cent of the wood used to produce printing or writing paper comes from virgin forest containing trees that are centuries-old.

─────────

Thanks to technological innovation, manufacturers now produce photocopiers and fax machines that can handle all types of recycled paper, and can also print on both sides. Urge your employer to invest in these; the money saved on paper will be substantial.

Sponges, Australia

Waste – Recycle old tyres.

Old tyres that have been discarded still have many years of life left in them: it takes 400 years for a tyre dumped in a landfill site to decompose. Every year, Britons replace 40 million tyres, weighing 440,000 tonnes. At present, 70 per cent are recycled but the remainder end up in landfill sites, although this practice will be banned from 2006. Alternatives to the rubbish tip do exist; companies specialising in recyling grind them down and convert them into material that can be used in industry. They can also be incinerated, providing the same amount of energy as the burning of coal.

It takes around 25 litres of crude oil to produce one new car tyre. Buy tyres from dealers who take part in tyre collection schemes and avoid those who do not.

Detail of tree trunk, United States

Agriculture – Eat fruit and vegetables in season.

How do markets and supermarkets obtain fruit and vegetables out of season? From crops that are grown using soilless cultivation, heated greenhouses or polytunnels, which use large amounts of water, raw materials and energy, or by importing them from countries where the climate is more favourable. In the latter case, transporting the produce uses considerable energy reserves (especially if transported by air), increases pollution and contributes to climate change. It takes 4 to 17 times more oil to transport food to its point of sale at a supermarket than it does to transport food obtained from local suppliers.

Eat fruit and vegetables while they are in season: you will find that they are of better quality and are healthier for you, and their cultivation has the minimum impact on the environment.

Pink flamingoes, Kenya

Water – Have your home fitted with thermostatic valves.

Water is essential to the survival of all living things, which makes it all the more precious. If no wide-ranging action is taken, within 50 years some 3 billion people in the world will suffer from water shortages. People can go without food for several weeks, but without water they die within 4 days. Access to fresh water has already become a vital issue in the 21st century.

To reduce your consumption, fit showers and taps with thermostatic valves. These are expensive but, besides providing ease of adjustment, they allow water savings of up to 30 per cent.

Death Valley National Park, United States

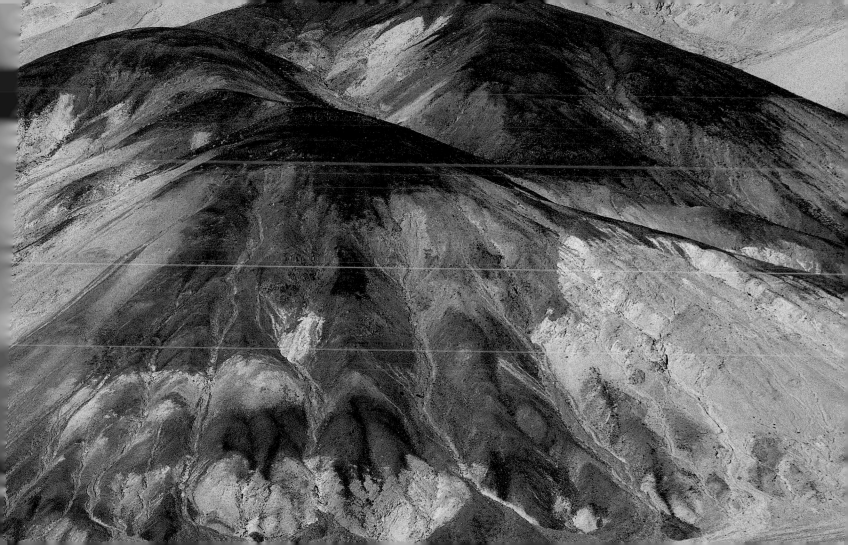

Lifestyle – Think about future generations.

Every year, US$800 billion is spent on arms worldwide. Almost none of the financial pledges made by the countries that signed the accords at the United Nations Conference on Environment and Development in 1992 have been honoured. By the middle of the century, the earth will be home to 9 billion people, making an extra 3 billion mouths to feed, all needing housing, heating and lighting. All this while 800 million people still go hungry, 1.5 billion have no clean drinking water, and 2 billion no electricity. By 2050, world energy consumption is likely to have increased by up to 4 times.

———

Other generations will follow ours. What kind of a legacy will we be leaving for them?

Glacier National Park, United States

Waste – Recycle aluminium.

Aluminium is extracted from bauxite in the form of alumina. Open-cast bauxite mining causes deforestation and destroys ecosystems. The conversion of alumina into aluminium also pollutes the water and air and consumes enormous amounts of energy. Producing recycled aluminium, however, saves 90 to 95 per cent of the energy needed to produce new aluminium.

Recycle your aluminium cans: they will be transformed into aircraft and car parts, as well as new cans. If all the aluminium cans in the UK were recycled, 14 million less dustbins would need to be emptied each year.

Yellowstone National Park, United States

Biodiversity – Buy products and souvenirs that encourage sustainable living.

During the 20th century, whales, tigers, rhinoceroses and elephants reached the verge of extinction and currently, several dozen more species are disappearing on a daily basis. Half the plant and animal species on earth could have vanished by the end of the 21st century. The market for the products of certain species – such as meat, eggs, feathers, or skin – is very lucrative and poaching has become a strong temptation to people living in poor countries, since it is often more profitable than working in a sustainable industry.

To discourage poaching, buy products that have been developed sustainably and for a fair wage in equitable conditions. When you visit a foreign country, find out what kind of products are produced in this way and seek out sustainable cottage industries employing native people.

Coyote, United States

Lifestyle – Keep abreast of your local authority's environmental plans.

It is important to keep informed about your local authority's plans for the environment in your area. Keep abreast of developments. Are their plans in keeping with a need for sustainable development, respect for the environment and a fair society?

If the information is not readily available, demand it! And once you have it, circulate it among friends and colleagues, as well as any people or organisations whom you think have a right to be informed and could be influential.

Mud spring, Kamchatka, Russia

october 21st

Consumption – Buy used, sell used.

By 2050, there will be almost 3 billion more people on earth than there are today. What will happen when the inhabitants of these countries also want to live more comfortably, buy their own car, use more water, or more electricity? The earth's resources cannot be increased at will, and we don't have a spare planet at our disposal.

Visit second-hand stores and car boot sales, and discover the art of bargaining to buy or sell items.

Namib Desert, Namibia

october 22nd

Waste – Replace disposable paper towels with washable ones.

Disposable products have been with us for years now. In this throwaway world, 90 per cent of the materials used in the production of consumer goods or their packaging enter the waste system less than 6 weeks after the product is sold. Do not encourage this waste of natural resources.

———————————

Are the towels in the cloakroom of your place of work disposable? Why not suggest that they be replaced by cloth towels? If you work as part of a small team, you could take turns washing them at home. This will benefit both the company and the environment.

Tassili n'Adjer, Algeria

Chemicals – Do not use chemicals to unblock pipes

Chemicals affect our personal health, causing asthma, allergies, cancers and reduced fertility, as well as the health of the environment. They disturb the reproduction of certain species, kill aquatic life, make wastewater even more difficult and expensive to treat and pollute the air and soil. Despite all this, scientists and researchers continue to come up with around 1,000 new substances every year, which are added to the 70,000 chemically-based products already on the market.

Most of the toxic chemicals used to unblock drains or pipes contain lye or sulphuric acid. They are highly corrosive and extremely dangerous. Instead, use a mixture of boiling water and baking soda and make good use of a sink plunger.

River, Iceland

october 24th

Consumption – Write to store owners and manufacturers.

The owner of a store is your main point of contact regarding the social and ecological aspects of the goods on sale. Customer demands, if repeated by enough people, always find their mark. Demand products with ecological labelling, Fair Trade products and goods with less packaging.

Write to the businesspeople who own shops and run companies to encourage them to take the environment into consideration when they design goods, and to favour the manufacture and distribution of environmentally friendly products.

Emperor penguins, Antarctica

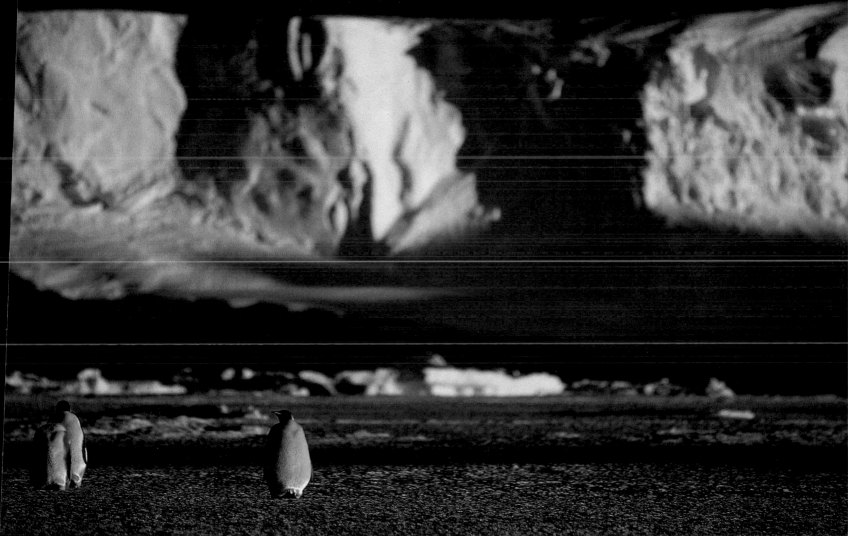

october 25th

Waste – Investigate 'zero waste' schemes.

An astonishing 80 per cent of what we manufacture is thrown away within 6 months of its production. Rather than focus solely on finding solutions to the problems our waste creates, we should think about how to prevent it in the first place, in particular addressing the issue of those products that are added to the waste mountain so quickly after manufacture. 'Zero waste' schemes seek to reform production, construction and consumption systems in order to address the growing waste crisis.

Look into the concept of zero waste and contact your local authority to see if it can be adopted in your area. Encourage your employer to do the same.

Lava, Kilauea volcano, Hawaii

Biodiversity – Discover the wetlands in your area.

Wetlands – the collective term for marshes, peat bogs, ponds, wet grassland and estuaries – account for 6 per cent of the earth's land mass. They filter out pollution and purify the waters that seep into rivers and underground reservoirs, while at the same time acting like a sponge, guarding against both flooding and drought. Despite this vital role in ecology, they are constantly receding in the face of pressure from human activity: urban expansion, development along rivers and coasts and agriculture. This is a heritage in danger: since 1900, half of the world's wetlands, including half of those in the UK, have disappeared. Over 500 sites across England and Wales are drying out from decades of water extraction.

The Ramsar Convention has designated 1,075 sites where efforts have been made to combine economic activity with the preservation of the natural eco-balance in a sustainable manner. Visit wetlands covered by the Ramsar Convention (such as The New Forest in Hampshire), discover their riches and learn about the threats they face.
www.wwt.org.uk/

Geyser, Lake Bogoria, Kenya

Agriculture – Discover Slow Food.

The Slow Food movement began as a response to the industrialisation of food supply and the subsequent loss of food varieties and flavours. It began in Italy and has now spread around the world. In 1900 there were about 200 varieties of artichoke in Italy, but only a dozen still survive. Today, the aim of Slow Food is to educate consumers about land stewardship and ecologically sound food production, encourage cooking as a method of strengthening relationships between people, further the consumption of local, organic and seasonal food and create a collaborative, ecologically-oriented community.

Opt for diversity and discover Slow Food. This international movement opposes the standardisation of tastes imposed by the spread of fast food. It has more than 83,000 members in 50 countries.
www.slowfood.com

Sequoias, United States

Transport – Have your engine serviced and tuned.

The 1990s was the warmest decade ever recorded and the hottest decade since the mid-1800s, when records began. The warmest years recorded were 1997, 1998, 2001, 2002, and 2003. By 2100, global warming will have brought about major climate changes. Forecasts vary, but the earth's average temperature is likely to rise by between 1 and 5°C over the next 100 years.

To avoid contributing to this problem, have your car engine serviced by a professional regularly. With a properly tuned engine, you will reduce your vehicle's polluting exhaust emissions by 20 per cent and save up to 10 per cent on fuel in the process.

Iceberg, Greenland

Waste – Choose packaging that produces less polluting waste.

New Zealand is implementing a zero waste policy, aimed at reducing waste at source and maximising recycling. Its goal is to stop burning waste and to reduce the amount that is dumped by 90 per cent by 2020. It would be good if all industrialised countries were to follow New Zealand's example.

Operate your own zero waste policy: when you buy products, choose those that are packaged in recyclable materials (paper, cardboard, glass) rather those packed in a combination of several different materials, including plastics. When buying yogurt and fruit juice, for example, choose containers made of glass rather than plastic, and eggs in cardboard boxes rather than polystyrene.

Lake Natron, Tanzania

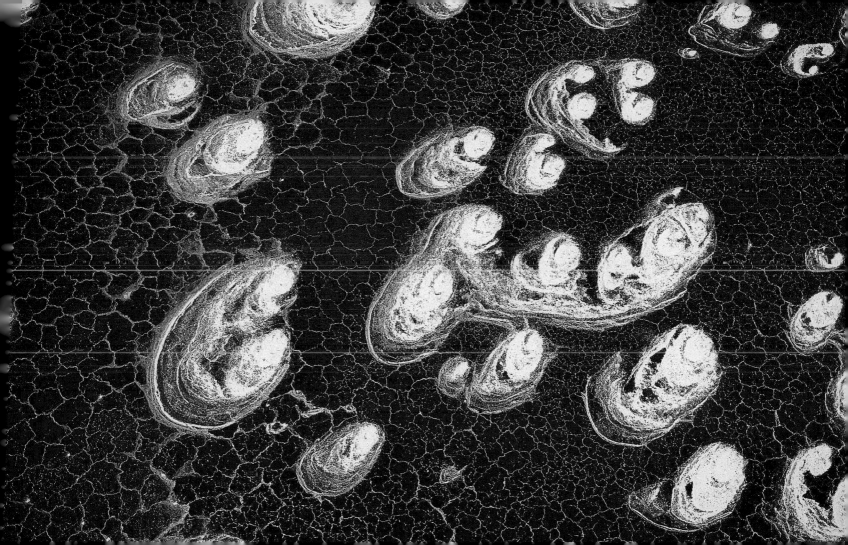

Waste – Recycle clothing.

Every year, the British public throws away over 98,000,000 tonnes of textiles. At least half of these could be re-used or recycled, which would help save some of the 5.7 billion litres of oil that it takes to manufacture this amount of clothes.

—————————

Give your clothes to charities or hand them in to collection programs. They will be recycled as second-hand clothes or as rags, or shredded and re-used as raw material (for textiles or packaging) thus saving energy and natural resources.

Scorpion fish, Thailand

Construction – Choose renewable energy sources for your home.

If a house is oriented to receive the maximum amount of sunlight, heating requirements can be reduced by between 15 and 30 per cent. Solar energy is accessible, free and can be easily converted into power to help heat the house and supply hot water without producing pollution or greenhouse gases. Geothermal heat pumps using the relatively constant temperature of the soil as a heat source (which is free, renewable and non-polluting) can provide part of the heating for your home and reduce your electricity bill. Most of these eco-friendly installations qualify for grants and financial aid. Check them out with your local authority.

Find out more. The energy information section of the Environmental Protection Agency (EPA) gives free practical advice on energy use and renewable energy. It will help to reduce your bills while protecting the environment.

Ice, Iceland

november 1st

Energy – Switch off your television and computer.

Your television uses as much power during the course of 20 hours on standby as during 4 hours of viewing time. Being on standby can account for up to 70 per cent of its total power consumption and up to 97 per cent in the case of a DVD player. Even 'sleep' mode on the computer does not save as much energy as you might think. It is far better to turn the computer off when it is not being used. A single computer left on all night uses as much energy as it takes to print 800 sheets of A4 paper.

Plug all your computer equipment into a single surge-protector for easy shut-down. And don't forget to turn off your desk light!

Aurora borealis, Finland

Transport – Use an electric car – quiet and eco-friendly.

Electric cars are well suited to city use. They are powered by an electric motor which runs on the electricity stored in special batteries. The batteries are simply recharged at a mains supplier. Cars powered by electricity are quiet and cause no exhaust pollution, making them an environmentally friendly alternative to cars with petrol or diesel engines. They are also cheaper to run: the cost of the electricity needed to travel 60 kilometres is a fifth of that of petrol.

In case you are still unconvinced, maintenance costs for an electric car are 40 per cent lower (there is no need to change the oil), insurance is cheaper, registering the vehicle is less expensive and parking is free in some cities. If your company has a fleet of corporate cars, mention it to your employer.

Talkeetna Mountains, Alaska

november 3rd

Lifestyle – Take action at work.

Various measures can be taken in the workplace to take the needs of the environment into account.

———————

Look at introducing a car-sharing scheme for journeys into work, adopting non-polluting and energy-efficient technology, waste recycling and the use of organic and Fair Trade products where possible.

Waterlilies, Venezuela

november 4th

Transport of goods – Buy products that are produced locally.

The abundance of cheap oil has made the world a smaller place. Products from around the world crowd the shelves of our supermarkets, plastic toys manufactured in Asian countries such as China, India and Thailand fill the toy shops, and every year world transportation statistics rise.

Think of the waste of resources and the amount of pollution caused by cargo aircraft and trucks, all contributing to the increase of greenhouse gases. Avoid encouraging the transport of goods over long distances; instead, seek out products that are made locally. This will help create jobs by stimulating economic activity and simultaneously encourage the development of shorter, less polluting delivery routes.

Basalt columns, Italy

Energy – Hot water, yes – but not too hot.

Up to a third of the energy used in the average household goes into heating water. The hotter the water, the more energy it requires; 60°C is usually adequate for bathing and washing.

———————————————

Check your water heater's setting to avoid needless energy consumption. Too high a temperature can also damage your equipment and plumbing. Water that is too hot is dangerous, especially if there are young children in the house.

Hot springs, Kamchatka, Russia

november 6th

Biodiversity – Respect the environment when driving an off-road vehicle.

Long before man appeared on earth, the mass extinction of many species had already taken place as a result of climate change, volcanic eruptions and changes in sea level. Millions of years ago, the most well known of these wiped out the dinosaurs and 70 per cent of earth's species. Today, species are disappearing at a rate that is between 1,000 and 10,000 times quicker than the worst mass extinction of millions of years ago.

─────────────

When you drive an off-road vehicle, make sure you keep to the designated tracks and do not go anywhere where their use is prohibited. The tracks should be wide enough to drive along without damaging the plant life growing along the edges and speed must be controlled in order not to disturb walkers and animals.

Sand, Algeria

Waste – Donate your old furniture and household appliances.

Some charities will collect unwanted furniture and old appliances at no cost. Some will even repair them and sell them cheaply, or donate them to low-income households. It is a good way of disposing of large items. Far better to find them a second home, than to see them discarded uselessly, destined for a landfill site. Remember that, in the case of soft furnishings, charities cannot take items that do not have a fire retardant certificate or label.

——————————

Rather than throw out your unwanted small electrical appliances, find a civic amenity site in your area. In the UK, contact the Waste Watch line for information on sites that accept white goods (cookers and refrigerators) and furniture that can be repaired and then donated to low-income households.
www.wastewatch.org.uk

Olympic National Park, United States

Lifestyle – Sign petitions – make your voice heard.

The amount of funding allocated to any activity is an indication of its economic importance or its humanitarian value. Defence spending worldwide is close to US$800 billion, whereas international development aid amounts to less than US$60 billion. World agribusiness spends US$40 billion on advertising, yet half the people in the world live on less than US$2 a day.

What sort of world do we want? Support public campaigns – sign petitions. Make your voice heard. By keeping quiet, we become the architects of global catastrophe.

Walruses, Round Island, Alaska

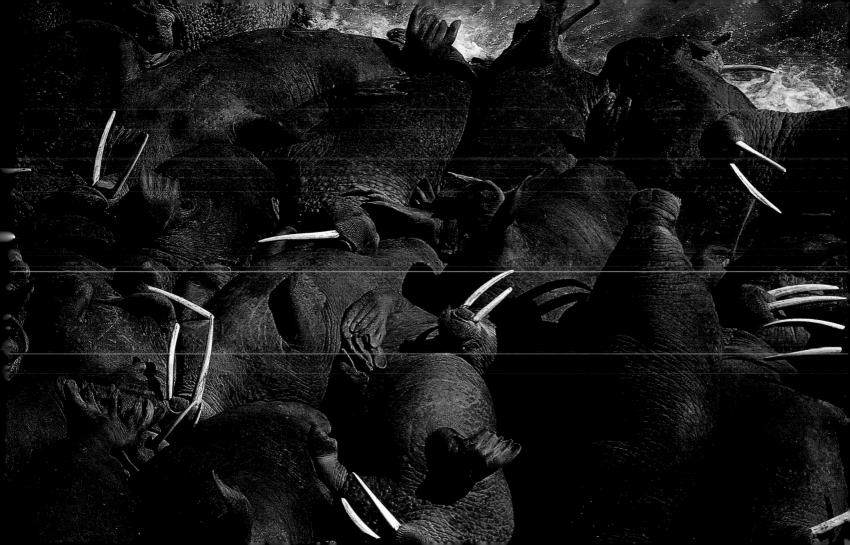

Consumption – Buy household appliances with A or B European Energy label grades.

Every product comes with an ecological footprint. Everything we buy draws on natural resources for its raw materials and energy for its manufacture, then releases into the environment the waste and pollution generated by its production and use. Present modes of consumption are therefore among the biggest causes of the rapid degradation of the environment on a global scale.

—————————

The European Union Energy label is an internationally recognised mark indicating energy efficiency. Various models of refrigerators, clothes washers and dryers, dishwashers, electric cookers and lights are ranked against a predetermined efficiency scale based on energy consumption in kWh per year. This allows consumers to compare the energy rating of different models.

Haleakala volcano, Hawaii

Energy – Do not leave the coffee machine on all day.

The list of energy-related problems makes grim reading: the stark inequalities in the world between industrialised and developing countries, waste, the depletion of natural resources, irreversible environmental damage... And yet energy consumption is rising inexorably, as are its effects – while we do not seem worried about leaving the problem to future generations. However, there are a number of measures that can be taken: technology can be used too make more efficient use of energy, renewable energy sources can be investigated further and promoted and we can all make an effort to prevent waste on a daily basis. We must also learn to live with less. All of this is possible without the quality of our lives suffering.

———————————

A coffee machine left on all day uses as much energy as it takes to make 12 cups of coffee. Switch it off at the plug, along with all electrical appliances, so that it does not deplete energy reserves when not in use. What have you got to lose?

Inlandsis, Greenland

november 11th

Waste – Don't bin hazardous waste.

Insecticide, weed-killer, paint, solvents (acetone and paint thinner), fuel and lubricants are all toxic, corrosive, polluting and even explosive. If you have any of these left over, they must be disposed of correctly, never in the dustbin or down the sink or drain. Left lying around, such polluting and dangerous substances could easily harm children and animals and contaminate the land or water supply. Treating water contaminated by these substances consumes a lot of energy and is expensive – and the bill is usually footed by the ordinary tax payer.

Contact your local authority for advice on properly discarding hazardous wastes.

Hot springs, Yellowstone National Park, United States

Chemicals – Choose low-VOC paints.

Paints used inside the home may contain up to 50 per cent organic solvents in order to render them more liquid and easier to apply. However, they emit volatile organic compounds (VOCs), which are diffused in the air and form a threat to health. Inhalation and absorption through the skin can affect the nervous system and internal organs, as well as irritating the eyes, nose and throat.

—————————————

Choose paint that does not contain harmful solvents, heavy metals or synthetic binders. They have minimum impact on the environment and on health, and their quality is just as good.

Tassili du Hoggar, Algeria

Energy – Encourage your place of work to conserve energy and invest in renewable resources.

The United States, which houses just 5 per cent of the world's population, produces a quarter of the world's greenhouse gas emissions. These emissions come chiefly from the burning of fossil fuels – oil, coal and gas – to meet the energy needs of industrialised countries. The United States has refused to sign the Kyoto Protocol, which is an agreement that binds countries to individualised, legally-binding targets to limit or reduce their greenhouse gas emissions.

Encourage energy-saving habits at work, and provide information to the management about investing in renewable energy.

Waterfall, United States

Waste – Sort through your rubbish to save raw materials.

For steel, aluminium, paper, cardboard, plastic, and glass packaging, there is life after the bin! Recycle these items and avoid wasting the raw materials and natural resources (such as wood, oil, minerals, and water) that are used to manufacture them. Aside from consuming less, recycling is the best way to reduce the amount of waste that is generated. Apart from the obvious environmental benefits, recycling creates more jobs than waste disposal and incineration.

————————

Do not let your recycling programme become the victim of budget cuts; let your local council know how economically and environmentally beneficial recycling can be. If no recycling programmes are available in your area, talk to your local council and your employer about making this important service available.

Maple, United States

Energy – Clean your light bulbs.

Clearly, by using less light and heating at home, you can reduce electricity consumption. If everyone does the same, demand on the power stations will fall, as will the use of the raw materials that are used to produce electricity and the carbon dioxide emissions that accompany its production... and their contribution to climate change. Conservation is cheaper and more efficient than technological fixes – changing to an energy-efficient compact fluorescent bulb (CFL) is a good way of saving energy, but turning the light off when not in use is even better!

————————

Wipe dust off your light bulbs – dust can decrease the amount of light they produce by as much as 40 to 50 per cent. Dust the bulbs in your home and improve your lighting at no extra cost to the environment.

Mount Rainier National Park, United States

Energy – Defrost your freezer.

Keeping food fresh or storing it by freezing it consumes a lot of energy, but freezers and refrigerators use even more electricity if we do not look after them. When the layer of ice in your freezer exceeds 3 millimetres, it is time to defrost it. When the ice is thicker than this, it begins to act as an insulating layer that can increase electricity consumption by up to 30 per cent.

_____

When defrosting, it is tempting to speed up the process a little by using a sharp object to hack at the ice, but this is not a good idea. If you make a hole in the cooling system, apart from damaging your freezer or refrigerator, polluting gases would be released into your home and the atmosphere.

Orinoco basin, Venezuela

Consumption – Demand products bearing certified Eco-labels.

The European Eco-label is an official recognition of the environmental friendliness of a product at all stages of production. It appears on hundreds of products, some of which are mass-produced. New categories are added to the list every year, which include shoes, paper goods, clothing, cleaning supplies, detergents, light bulbs, mattresses, domestic appliances, computers, ink cartridges, paints, fertilisers and even hotels.

————————

Eco-labelling is a voluntary scheme. Manufacturers who want the label submit their products for consideration. The scheme will only be adopted by more manufacturers if Eco-labels are requested by consumers. Ask for them.

Aïr massif, Niger

Energy – Choose your heating system carefully: consult a specialist.

Electric heating uses a lot of energy and is expensive: this is reflected in your bill at the end of the winter, especially if rooms are not well-insulated. If you are having building or renovation work done, now is the time to choose a heating system that uses renewable energy, such as a wood burner or solar heating. Among fossil fuel energy sources, natural gas heating is the least polluting.

To choose the most energy-efficient and least polluting heating system, ask a specialist, who will be able to advise on the best energy options for your home and your needs.

Gray whales, Mexico

Consumption – Be prepared to pay more for quality.

The combined effects of globalisation and consumerism often lead us to buy irresponsibly. Discounted prices tempt us, but how are such low prices achieved? Goods are frequently cheap because they have been made in developing countries on the other side of the world, where labour costs are low and there are no environmental regulations in place. Often of poor quality, the products soon break or stop working and have to be thrown away.

———————————

You get what you pay for. If there is a more expensive, but better-quality alternative, it is often wise to choose that. It should last longer and be more environmentally friendly because you will not need to replace it quickly, also saving you money in the long run.

Elephants, Kenya

november 20th

Waste – Recycle your computer.

Waste in the form of discarded electrical and electronic equipment – called e-waste – is increasing at the rate of about 20 per cent every 5 years (that is, 3 times faster than ordinary household waste). This could double in quantity within the European Union by 2020. In the United States, 10 million computers end up in landfills every year. Their toxic components – heavy metals and organic pollutants – are harmful to the environment and require treatment accordingly.

—————————

Some organisations will collect computers to sell them second-hand, or to give them to schools or humanitarian programmes. Donate your old computer to one of these, rather than throwing it away.

Ray, Australia

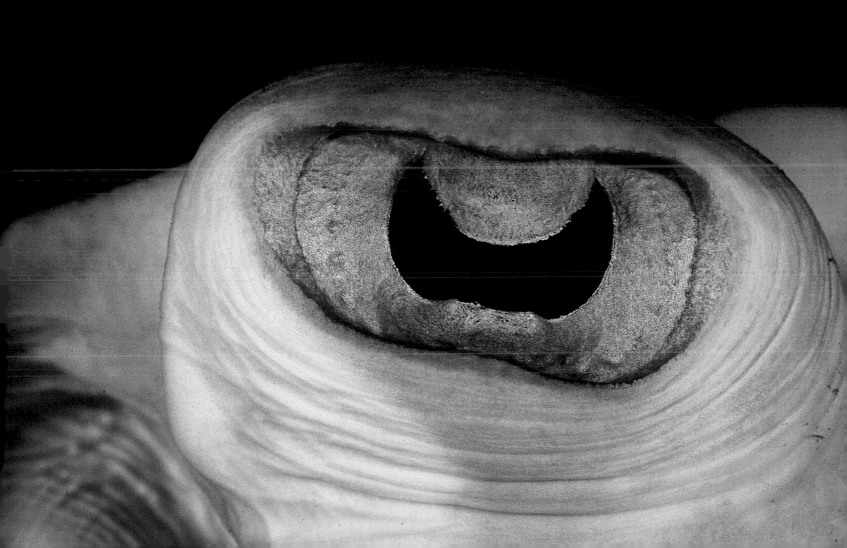

Energy – Your saucepans can save energy too.

Putting a saucepan on the cooker is something we do every day, yet even in this commonplace act, by paying attention to small details you can use less heat and thus save energy without changing the way that you cook.

——————————

Use pots and pans with flat bottoms – the larger surface area will make more contact with the heat source and therefore make better use of it. If cooking with electricity, do not use a ring that is too big for your pan, you would be wasting energy needlessly. If using gas, keep the flame low enough to cook your food correctly and not waste both energy and food by letting it spill down the side of the pan. When boiling food in water, use just enough water to cover the food – it is pointless to boil twice what you need.

Atacama Desert, Bolivia

Transport of goods – Say 'no' to guaranteed 48-hour delivery times.

A rise of 30 centimetres in sea level causes the coastline to recede by 30 metres. Scientists expect the sea level to rise around a metre over the next 100 years. This scenario, which the world's climate change experts believe is likely to become reality within less than a century, would completely redraw the world's coastlines, affecting both inhabited and non-inhabited regions : 6 per cent of the Netherlands, 17 per cent of Bangladesh and most of the Maldives could be submerged. Transport is the biggest contributor to global warming. If distributors were to be allowed more flexible delivery times, they could make full use of their trucks' capacity, or, alternatively, use less polluting modes of transport, such as rail and canal barges.

If you demand a guaranteed delivery within 48 hours, distributors will have to use their trucks in less fuel-efficient ways. Think first – is it really so urgent?

Mount Etna, Italy

Waste – Buy juice in bulk.

Two of the world's largest landfills, now closed, are set to become benchmarks in regeneration and environmental health over the next 30 years. The Paterson landfill site in Glasgow, Scotland and the Fresh Kills landfill on Staten Island in New York, are both slated for ambitious urban environmental renewal projects. In Glasgow, a million trees are to be planted over 230 acres of landfill over the next 12 years, which will make it the largest urban forest in the United Kingdom. Once the largest landfill in the world, Staten Island's Fresh Kills landfill is now set to become New York City's newest parkland. Its 2,200 acres will be developed into a park 3 times as large as Central Park over the next 30 years.

Help reduce the need for huge landfills like Paterson and Fresh Kills. A household of 4 people can drink more than 170 litres of orange juice a year. Buy this juice in the largest container possible and you will cut down on the amount of waste that goes to the landfill. Most recycling centres accept large plastic juice containers; some will accept wax-coated paper containers. Always check before adding a container to your recycling bin.

Stalactites, Greenland

Biodiversity – Do not buy a monkey as a pet.

Three-quarters of the world's monkeys live in the tropical forests of Brazil, Congo, Indonesia and Madagascar – regions where deforestation is destroying their habitat. Deprived of their shelter and hunted for their meat, monkey species are being wiped out one after another. Out of 240 species of primate, half, including the orangutan, are in danger of becoming extinct by the end of the century, while today there are just 300 mountain gorillas remaining in existence.

When travelling, do not get involved in the trade of endangered species and do not be tempted to buy a monkey in a tourist market.

Yellowstone National Park, United States

Gardening – Use organic methods rather than pesticides.

Chemical insecticides for garden use have several drawbacks: they harm all insect life, including the beneficial species that prey on pests such as greenfly, caterpillars and spider mites, and pollute the soil and water supply. Biological pest controls are an alternative, in which one living organism is used to control another. The natural enemies of certain garden pests, they keep pest populations below destructive levels.

***

Spiders, ladybugs, lacewings, praying mantises, predatory mites, parasitic flies and wasps are all examples of these helpful natural predators. Most can be bought through the Internet or mail order catalogues. However, it is important to remember that even such organic methods affect the natural balance in the garden. Before each treatment, make sure that the predator you plan to introduce will attack only the species that is causing the trouble.

Orinoco basin, Venezuela

Consumption – Take part in 'Buy Nothing Day'.

Since 1970, world production of goods and services has multiplied by 7 times. Over the same period, the earth has lost a third of its natural resources.

———————————

If you are weary of our over-consuming society, don't miss 'Buy Nothing Day' at the end of November, which is, according to organisers, 'the one day a year we turn off the economy and talk about it.' It offers an opportunity to think about the social, economic, and ecological impact of global consumption on the earth as a whole. If you're feeling particularly resourceful, hold your own 'Buy Nothing Day' once a month or even once a week. www.buynothingday.co.uk/home.html

Volcanic lake, Kamchatka, Russia

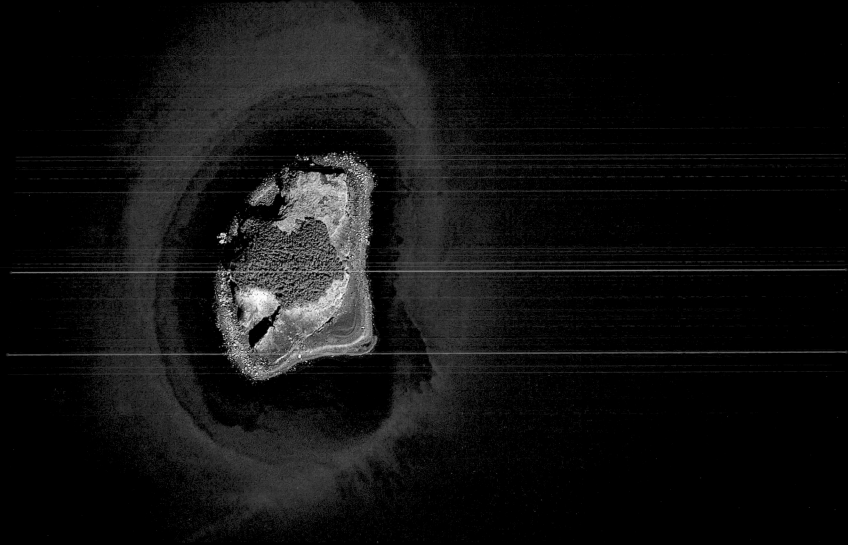

Transport – Take the bus when you can.

Global pollution, including greenhouse gases, is worrying because of its impact on the climates of the world. However, air pollution also affects our health: according to the World Health Organisation, traffic pollution costs the EU 161 million Euros a year. Cars are the biggest source of urban air pollution: each car emits, on average, 3 times its own weight, i.e. several tonnes of pollutants per year.

Fight air pollution by using your car less often. Take the bus: a fully loaded bus keeps around 40 car drivers off the streets.

Geyser, Kamchatka, Russia

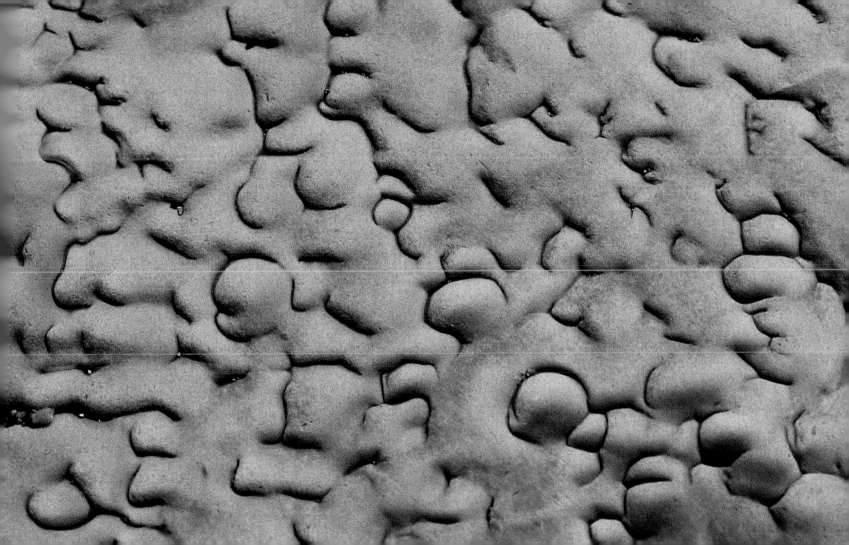

Forests – Do not smoke in enclosed or public places.

It is now common knowledge that tobacco is harmful to health. More than 3,000 substances have been identified in tobacco smoke, including carbon monoxide, tars, which cause cancer, and nicotine which causes addiction to smoking. Not only are smokers harming their own health, they are polluting their immediate surroundings too, creating a potentially harmful environment in public places . The damage does not stop there however: every year, over 3.5 million hectares of forest go up in smoke to provide space to cure the tobacco.

──────────

If you smoke, avoid doing so in enclosed spaces, and when you are in a public place keep to the areas designated for smokers. Better still, smoke less or not at all.

Hot springs, Yellowstone National Park, United States

Waste – Do not throw old spectacles away, hand them in for recycling.

In developing countries, millions of people suffer from poor eyesight and yet lack the means to have it corrected. Your old glasses could improve the quality of someone's life immeasurably. In industrialised countries, we discard thousands of pairs of glasses annually because we need a new prescription or simply want a change of frame.

The next time you replace your glasses, give your old pair along with their case to an organisation which collects and distributes them where can be re-used. Some opticians take part in collection schemes. Every year, more than 100,000 pairs of glasses find a new pair of eyes that they can help.

Kap Farvel, southern Greenland

Consumption – Do not throw away old baby clothes and accessories.

The birth of a child is a time of great joy, but it is soon followed by the realisation that having a child can be a very costly business. The long list of equipment and clothes that must be bought can result in a big bill, especially since most parents want to buy the best for their children. However, a large proportion of these clothes and accessories will be used for only a very short time.

To lessen the financial impact of a new baby, borrow from friends, accept clothes that are passed on by others, or look in second-hand shops. As the child grows, you can pass things on in turn. If the same plastic bath is used by several different families, it means that fewer baths need to be manufactured in the first place. You will be saving money and making an important contribution to the environment at the same time.

Lava, Kilauea volcano, Hawaii

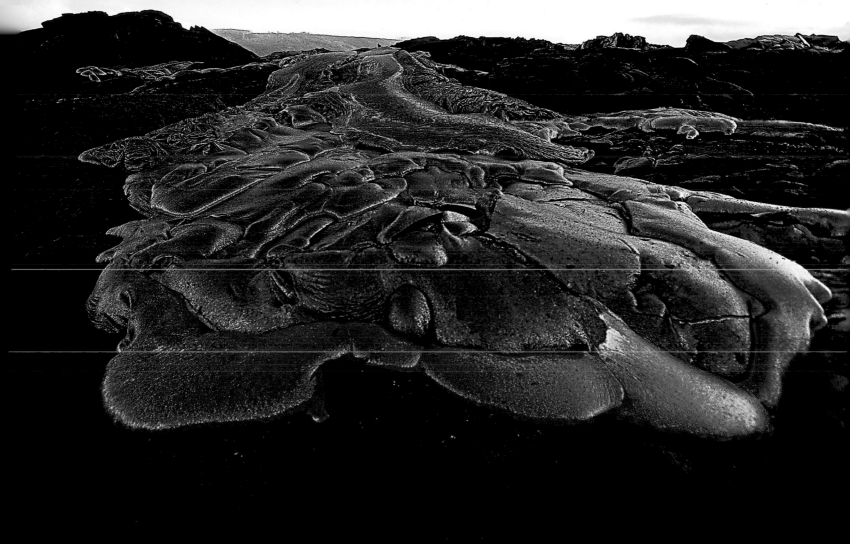

Transport – Do not use your car for short journeys.

Every large city in the world is suffocating because of the pollution caused by cars, oil-fired domestic heating appliances and industry-related emissions. Our reliance on the automobile for journeys that could easily be accomplished on foot or by bike contributes to the problem. Americans travel on foot only 5 per cent of the time, while Europeans and the Japanese make 20 to 50 per cent of their trips on foot.

Avoid using your car for short trips. Starting a car when the engine is cold causes a vehicle to produce the greatest amount of pollution. To add to the problem, the catalytic converter (which reduces emissions) is only fully efficient when it reaches a certain temperature, after a few kilometres have been covered.

Reflections, Alaska

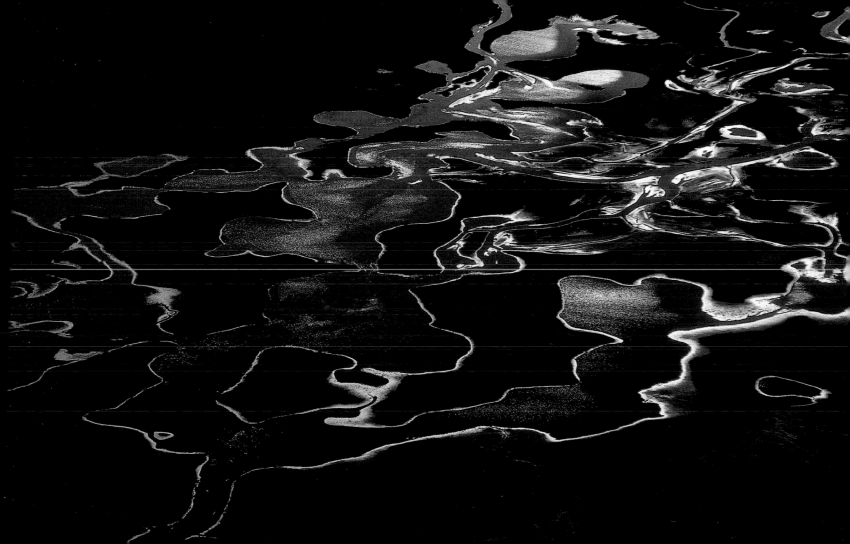

Chemicals – Use baking soda to clean the oven.

Between 1940 and 1982, the production of synthetic substances increased exponentially. Since 1970, world sales of chemical products have risen, from US$171 billion to US$1,500 billion. This vast market leads to the release of millions of tonnes of different chemical compounds into the environment. This pollution is widely implicated in the increase in cancer rates, in the loss of biodiversity and the destruction of the earth's ozone layer.

Household oven cleaners contain corrosive and toxic substances. You can replace them with a solution of water and baking soda, which is far less damaging to health and just as effective.

Tassili du Hoggar, Algeria

Agriculture – Persuade your workplace to buy Fair Trade coffee and tea.

In many farming regions of the developing world, earnings are too low for farmers to support their families' needs. Unable to make a decent living from the land, they are sometimes forced to leave it and join the swelling ranks of the urban poor. In other regions, they yield to the temptation to grow coca (from which cocaine is produced) or poppies (which produce opium), both of which will earn them more money.

By building more equitable commercial relations, Fair Trade ensures a decent wage for craftsmen and farmers, who can then live in dignity from their work. Tell your colleagues about Fair Trade coffee and tea, and urge your employer to purchase them.

Patagonia, Argentina

december 4th

Waste – Take biodegradable waste to the compost centre.

Composting is nature's way of recycling its own waste. Dead leaves, branches and plant debris fall to the ground and are digested by micro-organisms (bacteria and microscopic fungi). As the weeks pass, humus forms – the natural compost produced by this process. Composting carried out in specialised facilities gets rid of our biodegradable waste (fruit and vegetable peelings, garden waste) by transforming it into compost using the same process. This natural fertiliser, which can restore degraded soil to a condition in which plants thrive, is the reason why community composting is so important, given current agricultural practices.

If your local authority does not collect biodegradable waste, find a local compost centre. Encourage your local council to look at the option of municipal composting.

Indian summer, Canada

Energy – Set your refrigerator at 4°C.

Worldwide, the transport sector produces a quarter of all emissions of carbon dioxide (one of the gases responsible for climate change). Electricity generation by itself produces more than a third of carbon dioxide emissions, which rises to half of all emissions in industrialised countries. The appliances we require to bring comfort to our daily lives consume vast amounts of electricity, and sometimes waste vast amounts as well.

––––––––––––––

The ideal temperature for the inside of the refrigerator is 4°C. Similarly, the freezer should be set at -18°C. Each degree below these temperatures makes no difference to how well food keeps, but it increases energy consumption by 5 per cent. Keep a thermometer in the refrigerator and freezer to check the temperature.

Icebergs, Greenland

Construction – Look for BRE EcoHomes Ratings when buying a new home.

The homes of tomorrow will need to reach high environmental performance standards. The British Research Establishment (BRE) EcoHomes assesses homes for energy and water use, pollution, materials, transport, ecology and land use, and health and well-being. The EcoHomes guidelines encourage the creation of healthy and comfortable living spaces at minimal environmental cost. Environmentally friendly construction is not more expensive and pays for itself in less than 10 years, chiefly thanks to the energy and water savings it offers.

If you are planning to build or puchase a new home, investigate BRE EcoHomes standards. You can enjoy the satisfaction of turning to nature to provide your daily comforts, while respecting it at the same time.
www.publications.parliament.uk/pa/cm200405/cmselect/cmenvaud/135/4061612.htm
www.breeam.org/ecohomes.html

Emperor penguins, Antarctic

Noise – Keep your car's engine noise to a minimum.

Three-quarters of the noise in cities comes from motor vehicles. It is so pervasive that we no longer even notice it is there. A typical lorry passing at 50 miles per hour is 4 times louder than an air conditioner and 8 times louder than a refrigerator. Too much noise is bad for our health: it causes fatigue and stress, and excessive noise can even affect the nervous system.

For cities to remain pleasant or tolerable places in which to live, it is essential to keep noise pollution to a minimum. All car exhaust systems contain a muffler and you will certainly know when yours develops a hole! Have it changed when it becomes noisy.

Red ibis, Venezuela

Consumption – Replace your old domestic appliances.

The amount of water domestic washing machines use has been reduced considerably in recent years. With the advent of the European Energy label, consumers can now be sure that they are investing wisely. Savings are made in terms of water as well: An energy efficient dishwasher saves approximately 4,500 litres of water a year, the equivalent of the amount of water that 6 people can drink in the same period.

—————————————

Your appliances may have served you faithfully for years, but if they use much more water and energy than current models, it is better to replace them – especially if they are used frequently. You may have to pay a little more for energy- and water-efficient models, but the payoff will come over the life of the machine.

Erg (sand desert), Mauritania

Lifestyle – Encourage your employers to assess their environmental impact.

Naturally, companies, institutions and schools, as larger organisations, have a larger impact on the environment than individuals. As a result, when they choose to become environmentally responsible, their opportunity to make a positive impact is much greater. There is now a multitude of ways for companies and institutions to assess the size of their corporate footprint on the earth in a quantifiable and productive way. Environmental audits demand both long- and short-term goals, and specify ways in which companies can pursue more ecologically-sound operations.

———

Encourage your employer to commission an environmental audit. The chosen strategy can be a team-building and motivational experience for everyone involved.

Streams of lava, Kilauea volcano, Hawaii

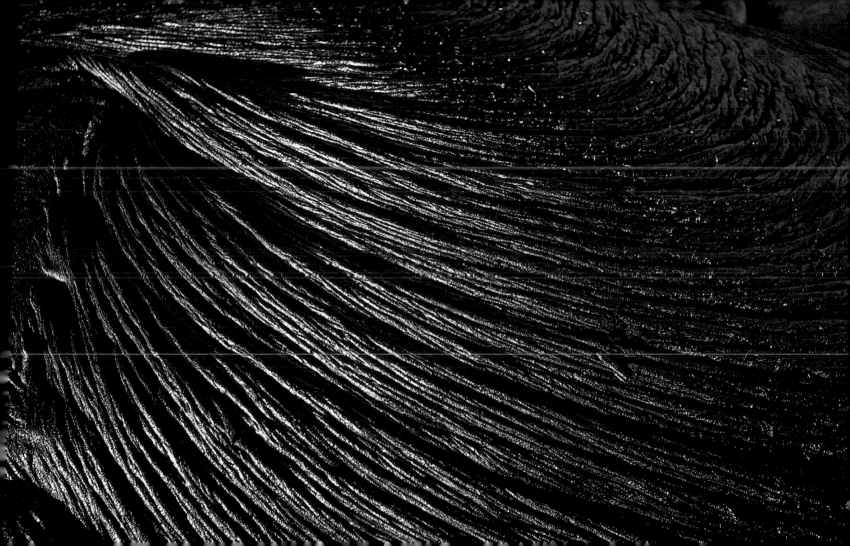

Waste – Use both sides of a sheet of paper.

Recycling a tonne of newsprint saves a lot of damage to the environment. It prevents the emission of 2.5 tonnes of carbon dioxide into the atmosphere, thus avoiding contributing to climate change. It saves 3 cubic metres of space in a waste dump. And finally, it saves enough energy to light an average house for 6 months. However, before recycling paper, remember that a sheet printed on one side only is only half used.

In the office, encourage your colleagues to collect sheets of paper that have been printed on one side only and that would normally be thrown away, and store it in boxes beside printers. Many print jobs do not require brand new sheets of paper, particularly when printing out drafts of documents. Both at home and in the office, use the reverse side of paper that has already been printed for notes.

Ice, Iceland

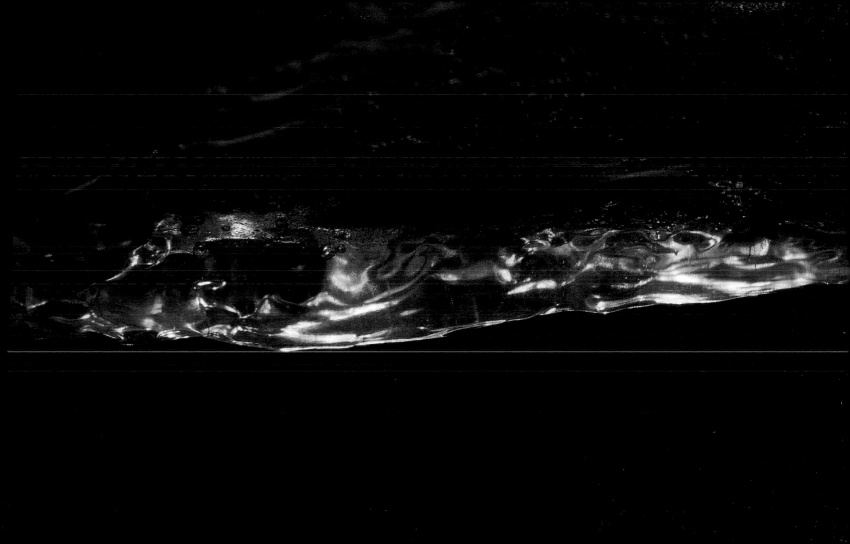

Energy – In winter, turn night-time heating down to a minimum.

It has been established that 80 per cent of the energy the world uses comes from non-renewable fossil fuel resources, the combustion of which produces greenhouse gases. Oil, natural gas and coal reserves are replaced at 1/100,000th of the speed at which we are now using them up. The exhaustion of these resources will probably prompt the rise of renewable, non-polluting energy sources, but we may yet have cause to regret not having developed them earlier.

––––––––––––

To moderate your energy consumption (and reduce your bills), remember that at night a temperature of 16°C is sufficient for a bedroom. To sleep healthily, as well as economically and ecologically, turn your heating down and sleep cosily under a good soft blanket or duvet.

Iceberg, Greenland

Lifestyle – Give a 'no-waste' gift.

You have to buy a gift, but the one you want is stamped 'Made in China'. It could have been manufactured under unfair working conditions. It will almost certainly have had a very long journey to reach the store where it is sold, involving the burning of fossil fuel and the accompanying polluting of the atmosphere. You will wrap it in paper tied with ribbon, both of which will probably go straight into the bin.

This gift represents much more than a financial outlay – it is also environmentally expensive. Why not give a 'no-waste' present instead? How about tickets to a community theatre, a voucher for a massage, or treat friends to a home-cooked organic meal? Alternatively, you could give up a little of your time and share the pleasure of a trip to the movies, a concert or sporting event.

Iceberg, Greenland

Gardening – Avoid total treatments.

Many chemicals that are regarded as harmful in industrialised countries are banned, yet many of these are on the market in developing countries where 30 per cent of the pesticides sold do not comply with international standards.

If you must use a chemical treatment in your garden, avoid total treatments. Lindane and atrazine are extremely noxious, killing all kinds of life indiscriminately, from earthworms which aerate the soil to insects and birds that help the gardener. They are harmful to people too. Read the information on the label and choose products that are described as being authorised for garden use – they will have less impact on the environment. Whatever treatment you use, if you have any left over, remember that the place to dispose of toxic substances is the hazardous waste disposal facility, not in the dustbin or down the drain.

River, Iceland

Energy – Keep warmth in by insulating your home.

Energy demands in the developing nations of Asia, including China and India, are projected to more than double over the next 25 years. Energy consumption has already increased massively in these countries: from 1980-2001, India's rate of consumption increased by 208 per cent, mostly due to rapid urbanisation and the increasing population. China's rate increased by 130 per cent. The world will not be able to meet this demand – the environmental impacts are simply too great.

You can make savings by improving insulation. On winter nights, increase the efficiency of your heating by drawing the curtains on each window. During the winter, if you do not have double-glazing, seal your windows with plastic or foam insulation or add secondary glazing.

Kilauea volcano, Hawaii

Lifestyle – Set a good example and educate your children.

The indiscriminate use of new technology, disregard for the common good in favour of short-term gain and the economic interests of private individuals or the state are what lie at the root of the world's problems today. It is the future generations who will have to face the consequences of our actions; we must not ignore our responsibilities as consumers and world citizens.

_____

Explain to your children that the western model of consumption must have limitations. Teach them to be concerned about the environment: be firm about saving energy, switching off the computer when it is not being used, turning off taps and switching off the light when you leave a room. Set a good example and practise what you preach.

Glacier, Alaska

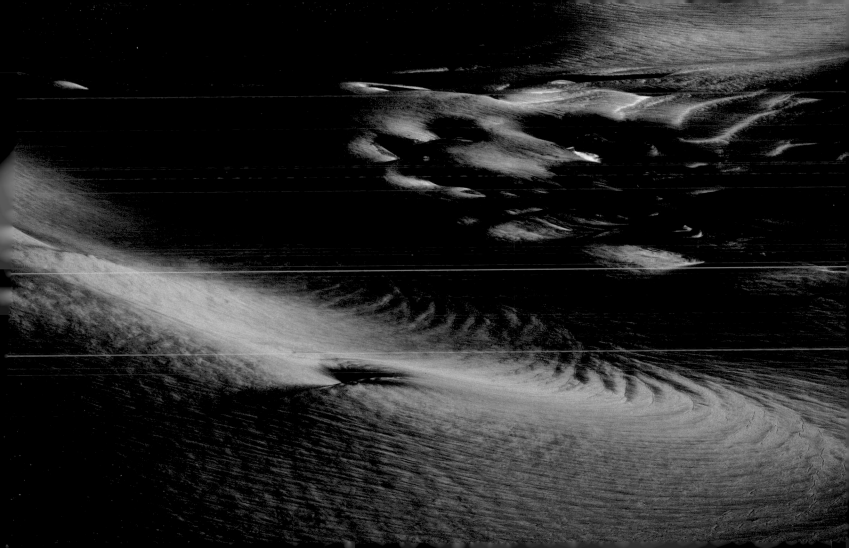

Water – Run the washing machine only when it is full.

Although intolerable inequality still exists in the world, the quality of life is improving for a growing number of people. However, as the standard of living rises, the more water each person uses. Our modern lifestyle does not use water sparingly.

A washing machine uses 190 litres of water per cycle. To cut your water consumption, only use it when you have a full load. When looking to replace your washing machine, invest in a front-loading machine: they generally use 40 per cent less water than top-loading machines.

Ennedi, Chad

Energy – Use wood for heating.

The forests of the United Kingdom cover about 2.8 million hectares, which represents almost 12 per cent of the land surface in the UK. Forests absorb carbon dioxide during the process of photosynthesis, storing it as carbon and releasing oxygen into the atmosphere. In the UK, the amount of carbon contained in our forests is equivalent to a year's worth of car engine emissions.

Burning wood for heating is more environmentally friendly than using electricity or gas. Think about installing a wood burner in your home, especially if you live near forested regions where the costs for transporting the wood will be lower.
www.forestry.gov.uk/

Geyser valley, Kamchatka, Russia

Biodiversity – Visit habitats that are threatened in order to understand the problems they face.

There are 12 national parks in the United Kingdom, encompassing forests, woodlands, wetlands, beaches and open moorland. While part of this land is privately owned, most can be explored on public rights of way – by bicycle or on foot. In the space of just a century, Europe has lost 75 per cent of its heathland, steppes and peat bogs. The coasts of Spain, France and Italy have lost 75 per cent of their sand dunes. As these natural environments recede, a multitude of animal and plant species also decline.

————

There are many organisations devoted to defending these natural habitats and the species that live there. Take part in the visits that they arrange for the public. Getting to know nature better and at first hand is a step on the way to helping protect it.

Red ibis, Orinoco, Venezuela

Waste – Switch to compact fluorescent bulbs.

If every household in the United States were to replace one light bulb with a compact fluorescent light bulb (CFL), it would prevent the equivalent amount of pollution to removing one million cars from the road. Though the initial cost is much higher than a normal incandescent light bulb, over its lifetime, a CFL will use up to 66 per cent less energy and last 10 times as long. The savings are unquestionable.

Specialist companies recycle fluorescent light bulbs, primarily for businesses. Fluorescent tubes are considered hazardous waste in the UK and may not be thrown out with general household rubbish.

Ol Doinyo Lengaï volcano, Tanzania

Chemicals – Protect the ozone layer.

Ozone is a gas that occurs naturally in the atmosphere. It is beneficial, acting as a screen that protects living things from the sun's harmful rays. In 1985, a 'hole' was discovered in the ozone above the Antarctic; it is more accurately described as an area where the ozone is less concentrated. Without its shield, both the earth and the people living on it are exposed to certain ultraviolet solar rays that can cause skin cancer and eye diseases, and disrupt the growth of plankton, a vital part of the food chain.

─────────────

An international treaty banned the use of chlorofluorocarbons (CFCs), found to be responsible for the destruction of the ozone layer. Make sure that the products you buy are ozone-friendly.

Clouds, Hawaii

Consumption – Celebrate Christmas sustainably.

When Christmas approaches, the developed world is gripped in a frenzy of consumption and people's resolve to be environmentally friendly is sometimes forgotten temporarily. A fifth more waste is thrown out at Christmas than during the rest of the year.

Why not ask your children to make some Christmas tree decorations? Rather than buying a plastic angel that was manufactured on the other side of the world and will soon be discarded, use your ingenuity and make your own from materials that you would have otherwise thrown away. You could also make a donation to a charity or give up some of your time to help one.

Lava, Kilauea volcano, Hawaii

Forests – Use less wrapping paper.

The tropical rainforests are home to more than half the world's plant and animal species, but every second, an area of rainforest the size of a football field simply disappears. Every year, almost 32 million hectares of rainforest are destroyed, while 137 plant and animal species become extinct every day. The statistics make grim reading.

Each year, millions of trees are pulped to produce the paper used to gift-wrap presents. Use ribbon or coloured string instead of sticky tape to fasten your gift-wrap; then it can be reused instead of torn up and put in the bin.

Grasses, United States

Consumption – Give Fair Trade toys as presents.

At a time when half of the people in the world live on less than US$ 2 per day, Britons spend on average £744 on Christmas gifts alone. Well over half of all toys are made in South-East Asia, (sometimes by children), with no regard for the social rights of workers, to meet the demand from rich countries.

If you have had enough of the kind of Christmas presents that serve little use, plastic toys and gadgets that soon break and have to be thrown out and packaging that contributes to the waste mountain, pay more attention to the presents that you buy for others. Look for Fair Trade toys and items that are made from materials that create little or no waste.

Denali massif, Alaska

Agriculture – Support organic poultry farming: buy an organic turkey.

Our food choices can encourage sustainable farming practices that treat animals humanely and encourage ways of raising them that respect their basic needs and normal growth patterns. Organic livestock farming does not allow the use of antibiotics, growth hormones, genetically modified organisms, or artificial light. It also supports organic agriculture, since the livestock eat grain and feed produced by such methods.

—————————————

Make it a rule to always buy an organic turkey for Christmas. Investigate 'heritage breeds' as well; producers of these breeds of turkey seek to put a traditional bird with more taste on your table, rather than the bland, all white-meat conventional turkey found in most supermarkets.

Bristlecone pine, United States

Consumption – Make your own greeting cards.

To date, scientists have recorded 1.5 million animal and plant species on earth, but they estimate that there are 15 million in all. However, several species disappear a day, before we have even had a chance to record their existence. Deforestation is thought to cause the extinction of a massive 27,000 rainforest species of all kinds, notably plants and insects, every year, while across the world every day, more than 1,300 tonnes of paper is used just to produce newspapers. Since it takes approximately 17 trees to produce one tonne of paper, it is clear why forests are vanishing at an alarming rate.

When you want to send greetings to someone, choose an e-card (a card sent by email), or one that is printed on recycled paper. Better still, be creative and make your own from recycled cards or recovered paper and other materials.

Glacier National Park, United States

Leisure – Respect the environment when travelling, just as you do at home.

The conditions in which tourists stay when on holiday in developing countries, with swimming pools, air conditioning and opulent accommodation, frequently divert natural resources away from the local people. However, in some tourist destinations attempts are being made to reverse this trend. The Seychelles, a group of islands northeast of Madagascar in the Indian Ocean, introduced a US$90 tax on travellers entering the islands. The revenue will be used to preserve the environment and improve tourist facilities.

──────────

Respect the environment and its resources both at home and abroad: do not waste water, switch off the light and television before leaving your hotel room, place rubbish in a bin and use public transport.

Namib Desert, Namibia

Waste – Learn to decipher the symbols on packaging.

A triangle composed of 3 arrows (known as the Möbius loop) is one of the most widely used symbols on packaging. It indicates that a product is recyclable or contains a percentage of recycled materials. It is one of a handful of international symbols supported by the British government's Green Claims Code, which sets out the standard of information that the public can expect to be given about the environmental impacts of the products they buy. Businesses use these symbols when making environmental claims about their products, although they can sometimes be misleading when it comes to packaging.

The difference between recyclable and recycled – or between what is possible and what actually happens – may depend on you, and whether you sort your waste. To avoid misunderstandings, learn to decipher the array of symbols and logos that appear on packaging, and ask your local recycling centre what they will accept.
www.recycle-more.co.uk/

Tassili n'Adjer, Algeria

Energy – Turn down the heat when you leave your house.

Contrary to popular belief, altering the heat setting on central heating does not cause extra consumption when the system is turned back up again. For every degree you turn down the heat, you will save 5 per cent on your heating bill.

When you are out of the house for a period of time, such as during the working day or when you are away for the weekend, turn the heating down 5 degrees below the temperature you usually find comfortable. When you are away for longer, set it just high enough to avoid freezing. Lower the temperature by just 1 degree on a daily basis and you will be doing your heating bill and the environment a lot of good.

Galápagos Islands

Lifestyle – Make a socially and environmentally responsible investment.

Through their trading links, some companies help to increase the debt burden of developing countries, favour the manufacture or sale of arms, or support dictatorial regimes. Socially Responsible Investing (SRI), on the other hand, looks not only at the bottom line, but also the environmental and social impact of your investment. SRI seeks out companies that demonstrate an obligation towards the environment and society and not just to the consumer; companies that develop working relationships with employees and investors; and finally, businesses with honest and transparent reporting processes.

Choose to invest ethically. Show companies that there is more to business and trade than the bottom line, that improving the conditions of the earth and our society are just as important as making a quick profit.

Rock painting, Australia

Energy – Install energy-efficient lighting.

Depending on what kind of light bulb you choose, it could supply you with 10 or 40 hours of light, or even more, all for the same cost. CFLs (compact fluorescent light bulbs) use between a quarter and a fifth less electricity than bulbs with a conventional filament, and last 6 to 10 times longer. Do not be deterred by their extra cost. Although they are more expensive initially, they save money in the long term – if you pay 8 pence per kWh for your electricity, a CFL can save you £20 over the lifetime of the bulb.

If everyone in the UK were to use just 3 CFL bulbs in their home, it would save enough power to supply all the UK's street lighting. If your house is already fitted with energy saving CFLs, make sure that your workplace and your children's school are too.

Ice floe, Alaska

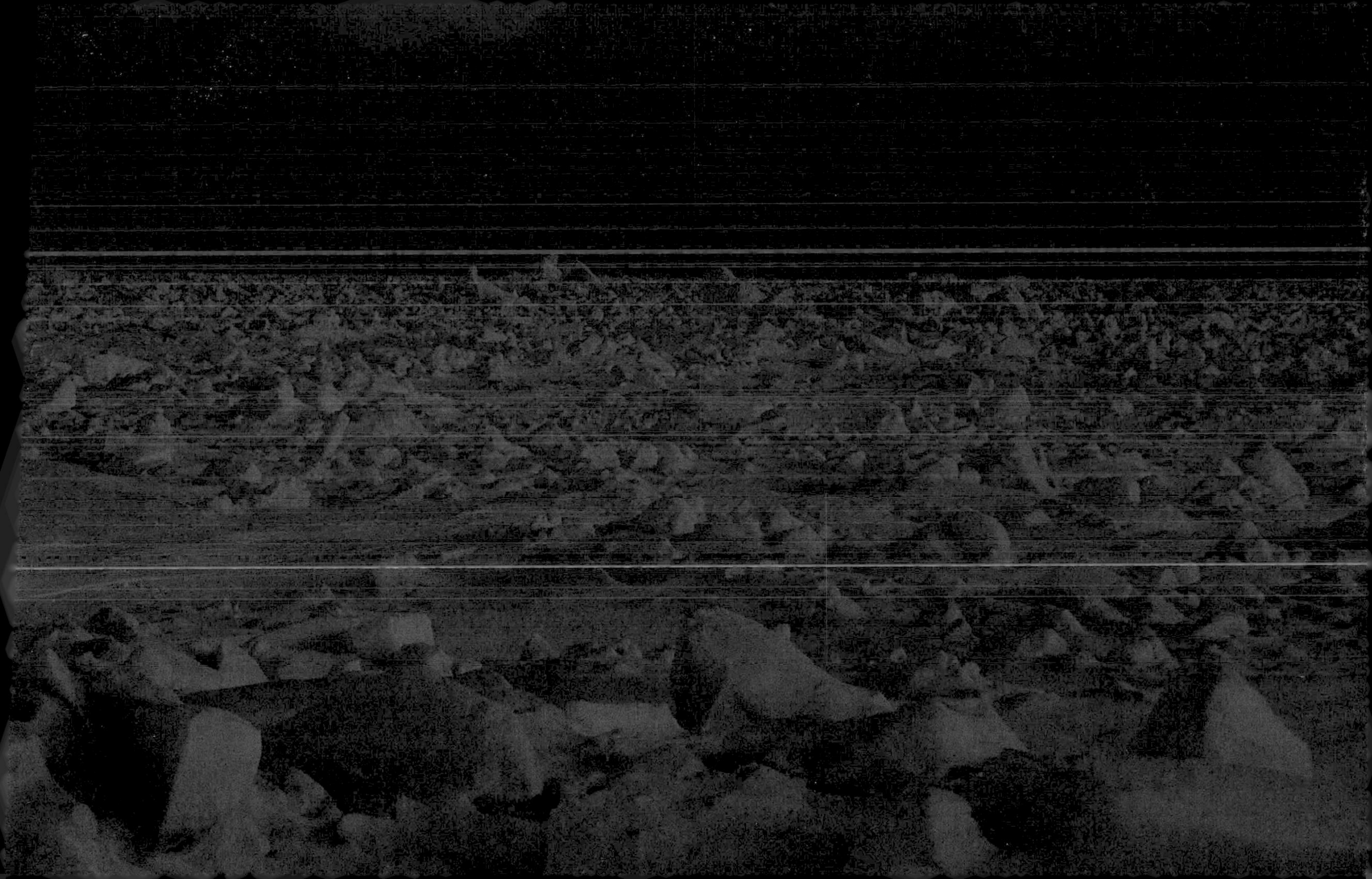

Consumption – Be a responsible consumer: choose your purchases carefully.

Everything we buy has a direct or indirect effect on the environment. When buying a product we must learn to take into account the following kind of questions. How was it made? Did its manufacture produce pollution? Does it use too much energy? Can the packaging be recycled? Does the availability of this product in my country mean the depletion of resources elsewhere?

Action to protect the environment can begin at consumer level, on the supermarket shelf or at the market stall. Think about buying items from local craftspeople – candles, honey, greeting cards. The closer you are to the source of the product, the easier it is to trace its ecological footprint.

Gray whale, Mexico

USEFUL ADDRESSES

ADVERTISING/ANTI-ADVERTISING CAMPAIGNS

www.mpsonline.org.uk (to remove your name from junk mail lists)
www.asa.org.uk (Advertising Standards Authority)
www.consumerdirect.gov.uk/ (consumer advice bureau)

AGRICULTURE

www.defra.gov.uk (Department for Environment, Food and Rural Affairs)
www.farmerslink.org.uk (promoting awareness of sustainable agriculture and rural development)
www.ifoam.org (International Federation of Organic Agriculture Movements)
www.viacampesina.org (international peasants'/small farmers' movement)

AGRICULTURE/BUYING LOCALLY AND IN SEASON

www.organicdelivery.co.uk (organic fruit and vegetable boxes and groceries within London)
www.whyorganic.org (organic vegetable boxes)

AGRICULTURE/GMOs

www.food.gov.uk/gmfoods (UK Food Standards Agency)
www.gmwatch.org (citizens' watch on GMOs)

AGRICULTURE/ORGANIC FARMING

www.organicfarmers.org.uk (organic certification body)
www.soilassociation.org (organic food and farming; certification)
www.slowfood.com

AIR

www.airquality.co.uk/archive (air quality statistics and forecasts for the UK)

BIODIVERSITY/BIRDS

www.rspb.org.uk (UK bird protection league)
www.birdlife.org (BirdLife International - the main international bird conservation body)

BIODIVERSITY/NATURAL HABITATS

travel.wildlifetrusts.org/ (wildlife excursions through the Wildlife Trusts)
www.english-nature.org.uk (Agency promoting nature conservation and protecting biodiversity)
www.cnp.org.uk (Council for National Parks of England and Wales)
www.jncc.gov.uk/page-161 (Ramsar sites in the UK)
www.wetlands.org (Wetlands International)

BIODIVERSITY/SPECIES

www.cites.org (Convention on International Trade in Endangered Species of Wild Flora and Fauna)
www.traffic.org (WWF campaign)
www.eu-wildlifetrade.org (guide to souvenirs made from wild species)

BUSINESS/ENVIRONMENTAL MANAGEMENT

www.businessandbiodiversity.org/ (resource centre)
www.bitc.org.uk (Business in the Community)
www.greenbiz.com/ (business and environment resource centre)
www.societyandbusiness.gov.uk/ (UK government site on corporate social responsibility)
www.iema.net (Institute of Environmental Management)
www.ciwem.org.uk/ (Chartered Institution of Water and Environmental Management)

CLIMATE CHANGE/GREENHOUSE EFFECT

www.metoffice.com/research/ (UK environmental and weather-related services)

www.ukcip.org.uk/ (UK climates impact programme)
www.nrdc.org/globalwarming/ (National Resources Defense Council)
www.greenhouse-warming.org.uk (fact sheets on global warming)

CONSUMPTION/CONSUMER PRESSURE GROUPS: ENVIRONMENT

www.environ.co.uk (independent charity working to improve the environment in the UK)
www. www.grownupgreen.co.uk/ (consumption, sustainable living, waste management)
www.beuc.org (European consumers' unions bureau)
www.consumersinternational.org (international consumers' organisation)

CONSUMPTION/ECO-LABELS

www.est.org.uk/myhome/efficientproducts/energylabel/ (energy saving trust)
www.eco-label.com (products bearing the European eco-label)
www.pitching-green.gov.uk/shoppersGuide.htm (guide to green labelling)
www.eu-energystar.org (office equipment bearing the energy star label)

CONSUMPTION/OVERCONSUMPTION

www.buynothingday.co.uk

CONSUMPTION/RECYCLED PRODUCTS

www.londonremade.com (recycled products and practical information on recycling)

CONSUMPTION/SUSTAINABLE AND ENVIRONMENTALLY FRIENDLY PRODUCTS

www.alotoforganics.co.uk (organic search engine)

www.ecomania.co.uk/ (online shop of environmentally friendly products)
www.ecover.com (environmentally friendly household cleaning materials)
www.getethical.com (ethical, organic, environmentally friendly shopping)
http://gogreen.cellande.co.uk/directory (businesses providing environmentally friendlier products and services)
www.gustoguide.co.uk (organic guide for the U.K.)
www.babykind.co.uk (washable nappies)
www.naturalnursery.co.uk (organic, fairly traded clothes and toys)

EDUCATION ON THE ENVIRONMENT, YOUNG PEOPLE
www.enviropedia.org.uk (research site covering 300+ topics on the environment)
www.cee.org.uk/ (UK council for education on the environment)
www.clean-air-kids.org.uk (for 8-11 year olds; information on air quality issues and recycling)
www.getwise.org (water and energy conservation programme)
www.fee-international.org (Foundation for Education on the Environment in Europe)
www.ac-grenoble.fr.yre (Young Reporters on the Environment)
www.eco-schools.org (European Eco Schools programme)

ENERGY
www.thecarbontrust.co.uk/ (advice on cutting carbon dioxide emissions)
www.worldenergy.org/wec-geis/ (World Energy Council)
www.est.org.uk/ (Energy Saving Trust)
www.energywatch.org.uk/ (independent watchdog organisation for gas and electricity consumers)

ENERGY/GREEN ELECTRICITY
www.greenelectricity.org/ (information for green electricity suppliers)

ENERGY/HOUSEHOLD APPLIANCES, ELECTRIC EQUIPMENT
www.energy-plus.org (refrigerators and freezers that offer the highest energy efficiency)
www.energystar.gov (Energy Star label)

ENERGY/LIGHTING, HEATING, AIR CONDITIONING
www.environment-agency.gov.uk (UK environment and energy use agency; practical advice)

ENVIRONMENTALLY FRIENDLY BUILDINGS
www.greenbuildingstore.co.uk (energy-saving, sustainable building products)
www.bream.org/ecohomes.html
www.greenerbuildings.com (resources for environmentally responsible building)
www.lowimpact.org (courses, information on low impact living)

ETHICAL CONSUMPTION
www.ethicalconsumer.org (brands and their social and environmental impact)
www.greenconsumerguide.com (environmental, ethical, sustainable products, services and news)

FAIR ECONOMICS AND LENDING/ETHICAL INVESTMENT
www.ethicalinvestment.org.uk/ (association of financial advisors dedicated to socially responsible investing)
www.uksif.org/ (UK social investment forum)
www.ethicalinvestors.co.uk (fund from the Ethical Investor's Group)

FAIR ECONOMICS/ETHICAL FUNDS
www.eiris.org/index.htm (Ethical Investment Research Service)
www.envocare.co.uk/ethical_fund_managers.htm (information on various ethical funds)

FAIR TRADE
www.fairtrade.org.uk
www.fairtrade.net (Fairtrade Labelling Organisations FLO-International)
www.bafts.org.uk (British Association for Fair Trade Shops)
www.traidcraftshop.co.uk (online sales of Fair Trade products)

FORESTS
www.fsc.org (FSC label)

GARDENING
www.rhs.org.uk/ (Royal Horticulture Society)
www.organicgarden.org.uk/ (advice and support for organic gardening)
www.gardening-uk.co.uk (links, gardening advice, garden shows)

INSTITUTIONS INVOLVED IN THE ENVIRONMENT
www.defra.gov.uk (Department for Environment, Food and Rural Affairs)
www.environment-agency.gov.uk
www.ieep.org.uk (Institute for European Environmental Policy)

INTERNATIONAL/MAIN ORGANISATIONS AND INSTITUTIONS
www.iucn.org (The World Conservation Union)
www.greenpeace.org (Greenpeace International)
www.panda.org (WWF-The Global Conservation Organisation)

www.conservationinternational.org (Conservation International)
europa.eu.int (European Union portal)
www.eeb.org (European Environmental Bureau)
www.earth-policy.org (Earth Policy Institute)
www.worldwatch.org (Worldwatch Institute)
www.wri.org (World Resources Institute)

INTERNATIONAL/UNITED NATIONS ORGANISATION
www.fao.org (Food and Agriculture Organisation)
www.unep.org (United Nations Environment Programme)
www.undp.org (United Nations Development Programme)
www.unep-wcmc.org (World Conservation Monitoring Center)
www.who.org (World Health Organisation)
www.unesco.org (United Nations Educational, Scientific, and Cultural Organisation)
www.world-tourism.org (World Tourism Organisation)

LEISURE
www.longitude181.com/charte/charte-en.html (responsible diving charter)

ORGANIC AGRICULTURE/ORGANIC COTTON
www.greenfibres.com (organic cotton clothing)
www.pan-uk.org/cotton/retaillinks.htm (links to organic cotton retailers)
www.patagonia.com/enviro/ (clothes made from organic cotton or recycled plastic)

RENEWABLE ENERGY
www.renewableenergy.com/ (news and links)
www.wrenuk.co.uk (World Renewable Energy Network)
www.solarenergyalliance.com (solar energy products)
www.bwea.com (British wind energy association)
www.itebe.org (bio-energy portal)

SUSTAINABLE DEVELOPMENT
www.sd-commission.org.uk/ (UK national sustainable development commission)
www.sustainable-development.gov.uk/index.htm (DEFRA department)
www.sci-scotland.org.uk/ (sustainable development site)

THE SEA/FISHING
www.msc.org (MSC label)

THE SEA/POLLUTION
www.blueflag.org
www.surfrider-europe.org (Black Flags)
www.mcsuk.org/ (Marine Conservation Society)
www.globaloceans.org (worldwide forum on oceans, coasts and islands)

TRANSPORTATION
www.dft.gov.uk/stellent/groups/dft_susttravel/documents/divisionhomepage/031336.hcsp (UK Department for Transport cycling page)
www.carclubs.org.uk/ (rethinking car use; car sharing links)
www.ctc.org.uk (UK cyclists' organisation)
www.ecf.com (European cyclists' federation)
www.eta.co.uk/ ('green' motoring organisation)
www.chooseclimate.org/flying/mapcalc.html (for calculating the impact of a journey by air)

TRANSPORTATION/CAR SHARING
www.liftshare.org
www.drive2day.com (car sharing worldwide)
www.freewheelers.co.uk/
www.shareacar.com
www.villagecarshare.com (how to set up a car share scheme)

TRAVEL/ENVIRONMENTAL
www.green-key.org
www.greenhotels.com (Green Hotels Association: international association of hotel owners who take environmental concerns into account)
www.eco-label-tourism.com (European eco-label for hotel and tourist facilities)
www.greenglobe21.com (certification of hotels, airlines, and travel agencies that observe the environmental standards of Local Agenda 21)

TRAVEL/ENVIRONMENTAL VOLUNTEERING
www.i-to-i.com/
www.ecovolunteer.org
www.workingabroad.com
www.btcv.org (British Trust for Conservation Volunteers)

TRAVEL/SUSTAINABLE AND EQUITABLE TOURISM
www.tourismfordevelopment.com (TFD label and Traveller's Charter)
www.responsibletravel.com (specialising in eco travel)
www.lonelyplanet.com (ethical charter, advice on responsible tourism)
fairtourismsa.org.za (promoting ethical, sustainable South African tourism)

UK/MAIN PRESSURE GROUPS, MULTI-THEME SITES ON THE ENVIRONMENT
www.panda.org (WWF-nature conservation organisation)
www.greenpeace.org (Greenpeace)
www.foe.co.uk (Friends of the Earth)
www.pan-uk.org (Pesticide Action Network UK)
www.encams.org/home/home.asp (UK environmental action)
www.sustainweb.org (alliance for better food and farming)
www.tradejusticemovement.org/uk

VOLUNTARY WORK

www.workingabroad.com/ (international volunteer opportunities)
www.timebank.org.uk/ (UK volunteer opportunities)

WASTE

www.recycle-more.co.uk (advice on recycling in the UK)
www.wastewatch.org.uk (promoting waste reduction, reuse, and recycling)
www.wasteonline.co.uk (practical information on different types of waste, composting, etc.)
www.envocare.co.uk/hazardous_waste.htm (hazardous waste disposal)
www.donateapc.org.uk/ (listing for individuals to donate unwanted computer equipment)

WASTE/BULKY WASTE, OLD CLOTHES

www.charityshops.org.uk/ (association of charity shops)
www.frn.org.uk (furniture reuse network; appliance recycling)
www.reuze.co.uk (recycling information)

WASTE/OFFICE, BUSINESS

www.icer.org.uk (Industry Council for Electronics Recycling)
www.itforcharities.co.uk (collection of out dated office equipment and all office waste)
www.oxfam.org.uk (computer and printer cartridge recycling)
www.paperchain2000.org.uk/ (list of companies that collect and recycle waste office paper)
www.computeraid.org (collection of computers to be donated to developing countries)

WASTE/MEDICINES

www.intercare.org.uk/ (organisation collecting surplus medicines)

WASTE/SPECTACLES

www.lionsclubs.org
www.vao.org.uk (Vision Aid Overseas)

WATER

www.water.org.uk (water industry information center)
www.ukrivers.net (news and information on the state of UK rivers)
www.britishwater.co.uk (trade association, lobbying group)
www.thames-water.com/waterwise/ (Thames water)
www.rainharvesting.co.uk/ (rainwater collection equipment)
www.greenbuildingstore.co.uk (domestic devices for saving water)
www.thames21.org.uk (charity working to clean-up UK waterside environments)

BIBLIOGRAPHY

Bartillat, Laurent de and Simon Retallack. **Stop**. Paris: Éditions du Seuil, 2003.

Bouttier-Guérivé, Gaëlle and Thierry Thouvenot. **Planète attitude, les gestes écologiques au quotidien**. Paris: Éditions du Seuil, 2004.

Callard, Sarah and Diane Millis. **Le Grand guide de l'écologie**. Paris: J'ai lu, 2003.

Chagnoleau, Serge. **L'écologie au bureau**. Paris: Maxima, 1992.

Dubois, Philippe J. **Un nouveau climat**. Paris: Éditions de La Martinière, 2003.

Dubois, Philippe J. **Vers l'ultime extinction? la biodiversité en danger**. Paris: Éditions de La Martinière, 2004.

Dupuis, Marie-France and Bernard Fischesser. **Guide illustré de l'écologie**. Paris: Éditions de La Martinière, 2000.

Glocheux, Dominique. **Sauver la planète, mode d'emploi**. Paris: Éditions J. C. Lattès, 2004.

Matagne, Patrick. **Comprendre l'écologie et son histoire**. Paris: Delachaux et Niestlé, 2002.

Ramade, François. **Dictionnaire encyclopédique de l'écologie et des sciences de l'environnement**. Paris: Dunod, 2002.

For children:

Durand, Jean-Benoît. **Protégeons notre planète**. Paris: Flammarion - Père Castor, 2002.

Jankéliowitch, Anne. **Y a-t-il un autre monde possible?** Paris: Éditions de La Martinière jeunesse, 2004.

Laffon, Martine. **Sauvons la planète.** Paris: Éditions de La Martinière jeunesse, 1997.

Masson, Isabelle. **L'écologie, agir pour la planète.** Toulouse: Milan Jeunesse, 2003.

ACKNOWLEDGEMENTS

I would like to thank in particular:

My editor Hervé de La Martinière for his loyalty.

Benoît Nacci for the pertinence of his photographic selection.

Anne Jankéliowitch for the quality of her research and her work on the 365 texts that accompany my photographs.

Catherine Guigon and Emmanuelle Halkin for their reflection and arrangement of the texts.

The team at Éditions de La Martinière: Dominique Escartin, Sophie Giraud, Audrey Hette, Marianne Lassandro, Valérie Roland, Isabelle Perrod, Sophie Postollec, Cécile Vandenbroucque...

Thanks to:

Everyone who participated in these trips at close quarters or from a distance: Claude Arié, Yann Arthus-Bertrand, Jean-Philippe Astruc, Jacques Bardot, Allain Bougrain Dubourg, Jean-Marc Bour, Monique Brandily, Yves Carmagnolles, Sylvie Carpentier, Jean-François Chaix, Carolina Codo, Richard Fitzpatrick, Alain Gerente, Patrice Godon, Robert Guillard, Nathalie Hoizey, Gérard Jugie, Janot and Janine Lamberton and the Inlandsis expedition team, Monique Mathews, Frédéric and Mimi Neema, Stephan Peyron, Philippe Poissonier, Gloria Raad, Le Raie Manta club, Margot Reynes, Hoa and Jean Rossi, John and Linda Rumney and the Undersea Explorer team,

Diane Sacco, Hervé Saliou, Vincent Steiger, Sally Zalewski...

Gero Furcheim, Gaelle Guoinguené, Jean-Jacques Viau at Leica who have followed me loyally for so long. I used Leica R9 and M7 cameras with high quality 19 mm to 280 mm lenses that are extremely reliable under all conditions.

Marc Héraud and Bruno Baudry at Fujifilm for their help and support. All the photos were shot on Fujichrome Velvia (50 Asa) film.

Olivier Bigot, Denis Cuisy de Rush Labo, Jean-François Gallois de Central Color, and Stephan Ledoux at cité de l'Image.

Richard Lippman's team at Quadrilaser.

My apologies to anyone whom I have forgotten to name and who helped me with this book. I am sincerely sorry and thank them wholeheartedly.

Project Manager, United Kingdom edition: JMS Books LLP
Jacket design, United Kingdom edition: Mark LaRiviere, Shawn Dahl
Design Coordinator, United Kingdom edition: Julie Delf
Illustrator: Izumi Cazalis

Printed and bound in France

United Kingdom edition
10 9 8 7 6 5 4 3 2 1

ISBN 0-8109-5977-1

Harry N. Abrams, Inc.
100 Fifth Avenue
New York, NY 10011
www.abramsbooks.com

Abrams is a subsidiary of